Hypochondria

Toward a Better Understanding

by Robert Meister

TAPLINGER PUBLISHING COMPANY
New York

First edition
Published in 1980 by
TAPLINGER PUBLISHING CO., INC.
New York, New York

Library of Congress Cataloging in Publication Data

Meister, Robert
  Hypochondria: toward a better understanding.

  Bibliography: p.
  Includes index.
  1. Hypochondria. I. Title.
RC552.H8M44   616.8'52   79-8700
ISBN 0-8008-4044-5

Designed by Jim Harris

To Patricia, my wife

CONTENTS

I. The Nature of Illness:
"Real," "Psychosomatic," "Hypochondriacal"

> *It is much more important to know what sort of patient has a disease than what sort of disease a patient has.*
>
> —*Sir William Osler*

There can be no proper discussion of hypochondria without an examination of the current meanings of the concepts of health and illness, which are befogged by many misunderstandings and fallacies. What, if anything, does it mean when one hears expressions such as, "It's all in your head," or "Asthma is always psychosomatic," or "He is *only* a hypochondriac"?

Most definitions of health agree with that of the World Health Organization that it is "not merely the absence of disease and infirmity, but a state of optimal physical, mental, and social well-being." Health is noncontroversial, sharply defined, lucid; even when we talk about "health problems," we mean illness problems. Health automatically endows one with a certain attitude toward life; by being healthy, one is making a stand; being healthy is problem-free and clean. Illness, on the other hand, has always been the subject of controversies and changing views.

The British Medical Dictionary defines illness as the "sum total of the reactions, physical and mental, made by a person to a

noxious agent entering his body from without or arising within
. . . an injury, a congenital or hereditary defect, a metabolic
disorder, a food deficiency or a degenerative process.'' This
definition is far broader in range and complexity than the one that
appears in one of the most widely used medical dictionaries in the
United States, *Dorland's:* ''A definite morbid process having a
characteristic train of symptoms; it may affect the whole body or
any of its parts, and its etiology, pathology, and prognosis may be
known or unknown.'' Moreover, it is immediately apparent that
the British definition comfortably accommodates hypochondria
whereas *Dorland's* does not.

No illness is caused by a single factor, although one factor
may outweigh all the others in determining a given disease state.
Causal factors include genetic predispositions or acquired vul-
nerabilities, as well as the individual's susceptibilities to harmful
agents and events, be they physical, chemical, biological, or
psychological. These causal factors vary in their respective relevance from individual to individual; the evaluation of their relative contribution to a given illness constitutes, ideally, the process of comprehensive diagnosis. The determinants of health and
illness always involve complex interactions between the individual and his total environment. Ultimately, the decisive factor
is the individual's evaluation of his perceptions and his personal
interpretations of them. In this context, hypochondria evolves in
the same way as do other forms of illness.

As early as the mid-nineteenth century, the French
physiologist Claude Bernard correctly saw illness as the outcome
of attempts at adaptation—attempts which, though *appropriate in
kind, are faulty in amount.* Since the adaptive response in its
intensity can be more destructive than the original assault, the
individual may thus be gravely damaged through the wrong
amount of his adaptive reactions. For instance, the presence of
pathogenic microorganisms in the lung calls forth immunologic
reactions that counter the invasion and do so effectively; but, if
these reactions are faulty in amount, they may lead to congestion
of the lungs and pneumonia.

Bernard's concept of illness as resulting from the wrong magnitude of attempts at adaptation deals mainly with primitive biological and neural levels of reaction. But illness in humans has a more complex meaning, since their attempts at adaptation are made not only to damaging microbial, mechanical, and chemical forces, but, just as importantly, to threats and symbols of danger, particularly as they involve relations to other people. According to Harold G. Wolff's theory of disease, under circumstances perceived as threatening, behavioral and attitudinal reactions serving to protect in a crisis may become *inappropriate both in amount and in kind.* When that takes place, functions which usually recur in regular cycles become continuous, and the tissues involved are thus pressed beyond their limits. In some instances, this leads promptly to dysfunction, to symptoms, to evidences of disease; in others, it leads to hypochondria or other neurotic processes; in still others, it manifests itself by acceleration of the process of aging. Under the latter circumstances, bodily illnesses commonly found in life's late decades may occur in the fourth and fifth decades and result in premature death.

The biological perspective has traditionally been the most important component of medical science, and the major part of a physician's training is devoted to the biological theories of body functioning and disease. Yet, even biological factors must be understood in the light of the environment in which they operate, which makes strenuous demands upon body functioning—the body adapting to these demands in both a physiological and evolutionary sense. It is fairly obvious that man's physical development and physical adaptations depend, in large part, on the demands his environment makes on him.

Biological adaptations to environment, namely, weather, altitude, and so forth, may vary from one physical context to another. Anthropologists have found that the Aymara Indians of the Lake Titicaca region in the Peruvian Andes adapt to life at an extremely high altitude. The Indians have developed large chests, great depth of respiration, and their blood is very rich in hemoglobin. These physical adaptations permit them to engage in vigorous physical effort in areas above twelve thousand feet, where we would tire rapidly because of the low oxygen supply. Similarly, anthropologists have described various "primitive" groups that can sleep in the open in extremely cold weather quite comfortably without clothes or blankets. Their bodies apparently adapt to conditions that would have fatal consequences to us. Man's ability to adapt to extreme external conditions is spectacular indeed, and René Dubos offers a fascinating discussion of some of these biological adaptations in his books, *Mirage of Health* and *Man Adapting*.

However, the body's accommodation to new threats and challenges in a changing environment may also be disruptive, because they cause strain. Thus, as the body accommodates to environmental changes, these adaptations also cause problems that result in illness.

It is undeniable that cultural beliefs have a profound influence on the health and illnesses of people. For example, many traditional Mexican-Americans recognize several illnesses that occur within their group, which they believe do not occur among Anglo-Americans. These conditions include *caida de la mollera* (fallen fontanel), *mal ojo* (evil eye), *susto* (shock), and *mal puesto* (sorcery). It is believed that "Anglo" doctors do not understand these conditions, and when they occur, help is sought from local folk practitioners. These conditions may be seen as superstitions by Anglo-Americans, but it is clear that they are considered to be important life crises by many Mexican-Americans.

Health experts who work in cultures other than our own have frequently found it difficult to convince people of the protective value of immunization, decontamination of water supplies, and other health measures, without reinterpreting these measures so that they fit local cultural conceptions. For example, health officials often attempt to persuade villagers in developing countries to build latrines. But, even when built, they are often not used, because they are inconsistent with traditional forms of behavior. Going out into the fields to relieve oneself can be both a biological and social event.

People in most cultures are oriented to the present rather than to the future. Thus, they are reluctant to undergo pain and discomfort to achieve some future protection against disease, unless these protections are offered in a fashion consistent with other cultural beliefs, values, and goals.

Our own culture has no less bizarre ways of influencing health and illness, nor are we less reluctant than others to make present sacrifices for the sake of future protection. As the most vivid example, we make vast efforts to publicize awareness of cancer and heart disease and propagandize for such prophylactic measures as self-examination and exercise, while at the same time we subsidize tobacco growers, and tend to accept the large-scale and heavy consumption of alcohol.

Medical texts and doctors themselves commonly speak of "organic" or "functional" symptoms, yet, from the viewpoint of the unified concept of medicine, the distinction is meaningless. As Wolff put it: "It is unprofitable to establish a separate category of illness to be defined psychosomatic or to separate sharply—as regards genesis—psychiatric, medical, and surgical diseases." The unified concept takes full cognizance of man's capacity for symbolic activity, which adds a crucial dimension to his adaptation to the social and physical environments, and to maintenance of health, as well as susceptibility to illness.

Every illness has both physiological and psychological components. The crucial question is *how much each of them contributes* to the patient's clinical picture. It may help the doctor in devising his treatment regimen to have a clear grasp of complaints that indicate *psychological distress, regardless of whether a physical illness is actually present.* The following classification is a summary of complaints or symptoms pertaining to the body, but indicative of psychological distress or disorder. Wolff's advice to the contrary notwithstanding, such symptoms are variously referred to as "psychogenic," "psychophysiological," "psychosomatic," or "somatization reactions"—all vague and loosely applied terms that have done much to confuse the understanding of illness in the minds not only of laymen but of physicians as well.

1. Bodily manifestations of emotional arousal, such as anxiety or anger, and of emotional disorder, mainly depressive or anxiety-syndromes, such as pain, palpitations, diarrhea, and so forth.
2. Bodily expression and communication of attempts to imitate a physical illness that meets the patient's psychological needs. This is called "conversion"—a Freudian term for the process by which emotions become transferred into physical manifestations. The typical conversion reaction occurs when the emotion in question cannot be either consciously expressed or even acknowledged. The result is a bodily symptom based on psychological misuse of the body part, but not on disease of that part. Therefore, *physical examination will demonstrate no organic defect* directly related to the symptom.
3. Anxious preoccupation with the body or a portion of the body which the patient believes is either diseased or not functioning properly. This, of course, is hypochondria, the main subject of this book.
4. Nosophobia, or morbid fear of a disease, such as cancer, venereal or heart disease, and so forth. This is very often and erroneously mistaken for hypochondria.
5. Severe bodily delusions, false convictions of bodily change, disfigurement, or disease, for example, of one's sexual characteristics having changed, or of having parasites. By the tenets of psychoanalytic theory, these express unconscious fantasies and signify schizophrenic or depressive psychosis. Nevertheless, they often appear in association with hypochondria.
6. Body image disturbance—a subjective sense of change in the shape, weight, size, position, and so forth of the body and/or

its parts. These may occur in association with schizophrenia, depression, severe anxiety states, depersonalization, and hypochondria.

7. The reexperiencing of memories of bodily symptoms experienced during a forgotten childhood illness, activated by a current psychological stress. This, too, can occur in cases of hypochrondria.

To understand why a physically ill or hypochondriacal patient feels and acts in a particular manner, it is necessary to gain insight into what his illness or disability means to him. For example, people who value their physical appearance highly are prone to psychological damage as a result of mutilation or disfigurement. To others, for whom intellectual achievement or perceptual clarity are indispensable conditions for self-esteem or pleasure, impairment of intellectual or perceptual functions by disease of the brain, or sensory organs, will disrupt the coping mechanisms. A man whose main source of gratification is sexual prowess is likely to be severely disturbed by impotence due to spinal injury, diabetes, or prostatectomy. Mastectomy, hysterectomy, or masculinization induced by hormones in a woman may well have similar emotional effects.

Such examples can be multiplied. In each case, the specific personal meaning of the disease or dysfunction is a crucial factor in determining that person's emotional and behavioral responses. In general, there is no organ or physiological function whose disturbance, damage, or loss could not disturb a given person's sense of security and worth, because of its personal, value-laden meaning. The psychological impact of illness or disability depends to a great extent on the individual's vulnerability as it relates to his personality and past experience.

From the psychological point of view, any form of illness may offer a solution to aggressive, sexual, dependent, or power-seeking conflicts that have been repressed. Illness may provide a legitimate reason for avoiding conflict situations and actions; it may also provide the rationale for either avoidance of or indulgence in behavior which the individual could not otherwise face or engage in without conflict. In some cases, it may satisfy a psychological need for suffering as atonement for unacceptable impulses or fantasies. When such factors are present, the individual may have a vested interest in maintaining his illness and react adversely to its improvement. His conscious view of the illness may be the exact opposite of his unconscious view of it. He may deplore in evident good faith that he is ill and clamor for relief and cure, while at the same time his nonverbal behavior may express the opposite attitude, which he is unaware of and may explicitly deny.

To some extent, illness colors the sick person's experience of his body, self, and environment, his values and goals. Many writers—notably, Proust and Chekhov—have written sensitive accounts of how the sick feel. While every episode of an illness is a unique experience, certain common features may be discerned. Narrowing of interests, egocentricity, increased attention and responsiveness to bodily perceptions and function, irritability, increased sense of insecurity and longing for human support and closeness are commonly reported inner changes of illness, whether physical or hypochondriacal. There is often an unpleasant change in the general body feeling, experienced as malaise. However, emotional experiences are not invariably negative. Some sufferers from chronic illness or disability experience an increased awareness of aesthetic and intellectual values and enhanced intensity of spiritual life in general.

The term "psychosomatic" is a very loose one. There is no agreement in the medical or psychological literature on its precise meaning. Some writers claim that there is no such thing as psychosomatic illness while others believe that all illnesses, even death itself, is psychosomatic.

Unfortunately, the term has gained wide acceptance by the medical profession, the lay public, and the media. It is generally understood that to call an illness "psychosomatic" means that it was caused by an emotional disorder or upheaval, and, unlike hypochondria, it is "real" in the sense that it can be clinically verified. The cultural and social norms that affect considerations of health and illness have established what might be called an unspoken "Acceptability Index" of various forms of illness. On such an index, bacterial pneumonia, which is regarded as a "real" illness, would indubitably outrank peptic ulcers, which are viewed suspiciously as being of "psychosomatic" origin, and all illnesses known to man would outrank hypochondria.

The acceptance of psychosomatic illness has its origins in, and is a simplification of, the work of the late Franz Alexander and his colleagues at the Chicago Institute of Psychoanalysis during the 1930s and 1940s. Alexander theorized that the bodily changes accompanying the chronic emotions associated with unresolved conflict would give rise, first, to altered function in the appropriate body organs, and, second, if long enough sustained, to disease.

Alexander undertook a series of psychoanalytic studies of patients suffering from chronic organ ailments and came to believe that every disease is associated with a specific unresolved conflict. He and his Chicago group studied seven diseases in all: duodenal ulcer, bronchial asthma, rheumatoid arthritis, ulcerative colitis, essential hypertension, dermatitis, and hyperthyroidism—a disease resulting from overactivity of the thyroid gland. Each of these conditions was associated with specific "onset situations," that is, emotional factors that affected the patient at the time the illness appeared.

Alexander also designated an "X factor," by which he meant a constitutional vulnerability of a specific tissue, organ, or system. Still, a patient may never develop the disease if the precipitating emotional situation does not occur, in spite of the presence of the predisposing emotional patterns and of organ vulnerability.

To illustrate, let's take a look at a few of the seven diseases, humorously referred to by some as "the Chicago 7," studied by Alexander's group. The central feature in *duodenal peptic ulcers* is the frustration of dependency desires, originally oral in character. The craving to be fed felt by the infant appears later in life as a wish to be loved, to be given support, money, and advice. This comes into conflict with the adult ego and results in hurt pride, since the infantile craving for help is contrary to the standards of the adult, to his wish for independence and self-assertion. Because of this conflict, the oral craving must be repressed.

The latently dependent person appears to be an independent, hardworking individual who likes responsibility and taking care of others. He responds to challenges with increased activity and ambition, works hard, and assumes greater and greater responsibilities. This, in turn, increases his secret longing to lean on others. To be loved, to be helped, is associated from the beginning of life with the wish to be fed. When this help-seeking attitude is denied its normal expression in a give-and-take relationship with others, a psychological regression takes place to the original form of the wish to ingest food. This regressive desire seemed to be specifically correlated in Alexander's studies with increased gastric secretion, which often leads to peptic ulcers. The crucial finding in all ulcer patients was the frustration of passive, dependent, and love-demanding desires that could not be gratified in normal relationships.

Colitis has its origin in very early toilet training and is a consequence of excessive demands for bowel control made by a parent. The infant develops inclinations to punish the parent for making demands that are beyond his capacity, but, since the parent is so much stronger, the punitive tendencies are directed internally. Punitive tendencies directed against the self—against the specific offending part of the body—result in destruction of the bowel.

Asthma also has its origin in very early life, according to Alexander's theories. The infant recognizes his dependence on his mother for survival. However, if the infant perceives his mother as cold and rejecting, he develops hostile tendencies toward her; yet, because of the possibility that the mother will respond by abandoning him, the infant is fearful about complaining directly and does so indirectly in a more subdued way—by wheezing. The asthmatic reaction is thus conceived as a partially suppressed plaintive cry.

For a striking example, George D. Painter tells us in his classic biography of Marcel Proust that the writer grew to believe, resentfully, that his mother loved him best when he was ill, and he tried to win her love by being ill. At age nine, returning from a walk in the Bois de Boulogne,

> . . . he was seized by a fit of suffocation, and seemed on the point of dying before the eyes of his terrified father. His lifelong disease of asthma had begun. Medically speaking, his malady was involuntary and genuine; but asthma, we are told, is often closely linked to unconscious conflicts and desires, and for Proust it was to be, though a dread master, a faithful servant. In his attacks of asthma the same causes were at work as in his childhood fits of hysterical weeping; his unconscious mind was asking for his father's pity and his mother's love; and his breathlessness reproduced, perhaps, the moment of suffocation which comes equally from tears or from sexual pleasure. . . . In early years asthma was the mark of his difference from others, his appeal for love, his refuge from duties that were foreign to his still unconscious purpose; and in later life it helped him to withdraw from the world and to produce a work "de si longue haleine" . . .

Alexander's theories appear exceedingly convincing, but the early optimism associated with his work in Chicago has faded; it has not been possible to establish scientific proof of their validity. Nonetheless, they remain speculatively brilliant and much support can be found for them in literature, if not in science.

One of the most famous cases of psychosomatic illness is that of Charles Darwin whose history illustrates the complexities of "being ill" in a striking manner. He was a tall, good-looking man with a healthy complexion, fond of outdoor activities and sports. His personal relationships seem to have been warm and simple and he had many devoted friends. Between 1839 and 1881, he published 21 books and some 150 scholarly papers—all rigorously thought out and beautifully written—which cover such diverse disciplines as geography, botany, geology, biology, zoology, and anthropology.

Yet, during all these productive years, Darwin was virtually an invalid. His son wrote that "he never knew for one day the health of ordinary men. . . . His life was one long struggle against the weariness and strain of sickness." He suffered from "fits of flatulence," coughing up bitter, fetid odors from his stomach. Many times each day he "retched and vomited," bringing up "acid, slime, and clots of blood." The attacks were accompanied by headaches, dizziness, shivering, sinking sensations, and palpitations of the heart. He was insomniac and "chronically exhausted." His skin erupted from time to time with boils, rashes, and eczema, and he was hardly recognizable during these attacks. Darwin himself cataloged his symptoms in his *Diary of Health,* and he went from doctor to doctor, trying every available Victorian cure from mesmerism to hydropathy. None worked for long, and he remained miserably ill and has been undiagnosed to this day.

Medical explanations directed to the symptoms have been as numerous over the years as the symptoms themselves, and included chronic brucellosis (also known as undulant fever or goat fever), Chagas' disease (a parasitic infection prevalent in South America where Darwin was bitten by a "great black bug" in 1835), gout, malaria, narcolepsy, hyperinsulinism, and porphyria (an inherited metabolic disease), among many others. Although all these diagnoses have been ruled out over the years, no authoritative medical explanation has yet been presented. As recently as 1971, a prominent anthropologist proposed that Darwin suffered from chronic arsenic poisoning—which might explain his ruddy complexion but almost nothing else.

A variety of psychological explanations have also been offered, ranging from neurasthenia to severe anxiety neurosis in an obsessional character, but they agree only on the point that Darwin must have had repressed hostility to his father—even though his abundant letters and memoirs reveal no evidence of it. There is also no evidence for the seemingly plausible suggestion that Darwin had repressed hostility to his wife, though his major symptoms appeared almost immediately after his marriage.

The most recent psychological explanation states that Darwin's illness was rooted in his work on evolutionary theory which coincided with the abandonment of his religious beliefs. It is a matter of record that his illness was at its worst during his work on that subject and that he never consciously faced the psychological consequences of having abandoned Christianity. "I have never tried looking into my own mind," he confessed while at the same time he was retching, vomiting, and trembling each day. Undaunted by lack of solid evidence, it is tempting to speculate that guilt over his abandoned faith was the principal mechanism of his profound suffering.

Psychosomatic illnesses can be generated not only in individuals and family groups, but also on a mass scale in the form of epidemics, or "mental plagues," as they were called by Hecker in his classic work, *The Epidemics of the Middle Ages*. The "dancing mania," which included "tarantism" in Italy, as well as St. John's and St. Vitus's dances in the north, is one of the best documented psychic epidemics. This strange affliction, characterized by wild dancing, screaming, bodily distortions, mental aberration, abdominal pain, and even convulsions, affected entire communities between 1374 and the beginning of the seventeenth century. Hecker reports that at one time it affected five hundred inhabitants of Cologne and that the streets of Metz were filled with over one thousand dancers. In discussing the causes of this phenomenon, he mentions that the wretched and oppressed populace had been subjected to great natural disasters, such as the recent wave of the Black Death, famines, and "the incessant feuds of the barons," which resulted in miserable conditions and the corruption of morals.

During the fifteenth century, there were sporadic occurrences of compulsive or continuous dancing, but all involved single individuals. Then, in 1518, a great epidemic of continuous dancing broke out in Strasbourg. The scholarly medical historian George Rosen offered this account:

> Eight days before the feast of Mary Magdalene a woman began to dance, and after this went on for some four to six days she was sent to the chapel of St. Vitus at Hohlenstein, near Zabern. Soon thereafter more dancers appeared and the number grew until more than a hundred danced at a time. Eventually the municipal council forbade all public gatherings and music, restricted the dancers to two guild halls, and then sent them off to the chapel of St. Vitus. According to one account, more than four hundred people were affected within four weeks. Various chroniclers point out that this was a period of ruined harvests, severe famine, general want, and widespread disease. This was also the time of the early Reformation and thus of religious unrest.

Tarantism was especially prevalent in southern Italy from the fifteenth to the seventeenth centuries, and nobody doubted at the time that it was caused by the bite of the tarantula, a ground spider commonly found in southeast Italy. Those affected, Hecker tells us,

> generally fell into a state of melancholy, and appeared to be stupefied, and scarcely in possession of their senses. This condition was, in many cases, united with so great a sensibility to music, that, at the very first tones of their favorite melodies, they sprang up, shouting for joy, and danced on without intermission, until they sank to the ground exhausted and almost lifeless. In others, the disease did not take this cheerful turn. They wept constantly, and as if pining away with some unsatisfied desire, spent their days in the greatest misery and anxiety. Others again, in morbid fits of love, cast their longing looks on women, and instances of death are recorded, which are said to have occurred under a paroxysm of either laughing or weeping.

It was widely believed that music and dancing distributed the poison of the tarantula over the whole body and expelled it through the skin. (Let it be noted that as recently as 1963 an outbreak of hysteria associated with fears of having been bitten by insects was reported among workers in a textile plant in South Carolina.)

On August 22, 1485, Henry VII became the first Tudor king of England by defeating the forces of Richard III in a short battle at Bosworth Field. But, Macaulay tells us, "the joy of the nation was clouded by a mortal disease which thinned the ranks of the warriors, and following in the rear of Henry's victorious army, spread in a few weeks from the distant mountains of Wales to the metropolis of the empire." This epidemical disease, "the sweating sickness," hit England on five separate occasions between 1485 and 1551—spreading to northern Europe only once in 1529—and never returned afterward. According to a contemporary chronicler, "a fatal sweat attacked the body, wracking it with pains in the head and stomach; moreover there was a terrible sensation of heat."

This mysterious disease was aggravated by the unfortunate delusion that whoever wished to escape death when hit with this particularly English pestilence must sweat for twenty-four hours without interruption. So they put the patient in bed, covered him with feather beds and furs, fired up the stove, closed all windows, and to make sure that he remained covered, members of his household lay on top of him. He couldn't even move his hands or feet, and, bathed in agonizing sweat, usually gave up the ghost.

The mental shock sustained by European nations during the Black Plague is without parallel and beyond description and caused many "mental epidemics," such as the dancing mania and the sweating sickness, but it should not be thought that these epidemics took place before the seventeenth century only. In 1955, an epidemic occurred at the Royal Free Hospital in London. Over three hundred staff members—not patients—became ill with severe malaise, slight fever, and bizarre neurological symptoms. The outbreak recurred about fifteen times. During the 1960s a number of outbreaks of epidemic hysteria were reported in the United States and Britain, particularly among high-school students, and comparable epidemics have also been reported in non-Western regions, such as Taiwan and East Africa. It has been suggested that occurrences of this nature do not happen unless there are restraints to be reduced; thus, mental epidemics occur not only at times when unfavorable social conditions are conducive to their outbreak, but also at times when repression is present. From this point of view, the epidemic of hysteria described by Aldous Huxley in his masterful study, *The Devils of Loudon*, can be seen as a miscarried revolt against the sexual repression of that time.

It is not possible to conclude a discussion of psychosomatic illness without some observations about the mind-body dichotomy and interaction. The view that body and mind are separate parts of man is strictly a Western one and as old as written history; its codification by Descartes produced hopeless confusion which has affected psychiatry more than any other field. Mythologies, religions, and philosophies have been concerned with the relationship of body to mind, but different ages and different thinkers evaluated it differently. The Platonic notion was that the mind rules over the body, which is but the executor of desires and ideas. Hippocrates, on the other hand, considered psychological processes nothing but "epiphenomena," insignificant reflections of bodily processes which themselves are subject to the universal laws of the physical universe.

Ultimately, the blame for the confusion befogging the subject must be laid at the doorstep of Christianity, or, more precisely, Judeo-Christianity. Contempt for the body, a singularly odious tenet of Judeo-Christianity, was the source from which theories of the mind and the consequent split between it and the body evolved. The fact that the pendulum has swung and at the present time the body and every indulgence therefor is the fashion of the day alters nothing; it simply dramatizes the continuing existence of the split.

It may have been the original intent of psychosomatic medicine to extend into the mind-body problem with the purpose of dissolving it, but the very term "psychosomatic" was predictive of the eventual failure of that intent. Aside from turning out to be a scientific disappointment which failed to introduce the criterion of predictability into large areas of medicine, it succeeded lamentably in injecting the problem into public, even popular, consciousness, which does not exclude that of many physicians. In practical terms, when a physician views an illness as psychosomatic or hypochondriacal, the treatment he provides, if he provides any at all, is more likely to be less scientific, less specific, than the treatment designed for what is viewed as a "real" illness. In all too many cases, patients are dismissed with the remark, "It's only psychosomatic," and a prescription for a tranquilizer.

Medical thinkers in earlier times were more prudent about the unity of mind and body than we are. In 1764, Robert Whytt wrote:

> Nothing produces more sudden or surprising changes in the body than violent affections of the mind, whether these be excited by external objects, or by the exercise of internal sense.

In 1840, Laycock declared: "The whole of the relations of the mind to the body require a thorough revision." And in his classic *Insanity in Ancient and Modern Life,* Daniel Hack Tuke wrote in 1878:

> Man must be viewed, then, his nature must be treated, as a compound of nerve, vessels, life, mind. He must be studied as a symmetrical whole. One design, one ultimate law, unites all the parts of which he is composed. Their connection and interdependence must be clearly seen, understood, and, most important of all, acted upon.

It is, of course, indisputable that we are indivisible organisms. Bodily reactions to emotions are among the most common experiences of life. One feels afraid: the pulse becomes faster and breathing deeper. One feels anger: the face flushes and muscles tense. One feels disgust: the stomach begins to churn. Laughter makes our diaphragm go into spasmodic contractions, our facial muscles contort; a tragic event causes our lachrymal glands to secrete tears and we weep.

Subjective sensations, such as fear, anger, disgust, merriment, and sorrow mobilize highly complex bodily processes; changes take place in the heart rate and blood circulation, in respiration, in stomach and bowel activity, in the musculoskeletal system, and in the glands. Conversely, bodily changes have a comparable effect on our psychology. We drink alcohol, thereby changing our body chemistry, and we promptly react with changes in mood. Sedatives have certain physiological effects and, as a result, we feel sleepy. Thus, in some events the first links are perceived subjectively and the subsequent links are objectively measurable as changes in body functions. In other events, the first links are objectively measurable, such as the amount of alcohol we drink, and the subsequent ones are subjective.

In sum, it seems prudent to regard the separation of the individual into body and mind and the concomitant divisions of medicine as often dangerous fallacies of Western civilization. As this book will attempt to demonstrate, the neglect and misunderstanding of hypochrondria are direct results of these fallacies, which were introduced into medicine with the expanding use of allegory, analogy, metaphor, and simile, popularized in the twentieth century by Freudian psychology. As Dutch historian Johan Huizinga has pointed out, analogical thinking establishes direct connections between phenomena without statistical validation of their concomitance, and without acknowledgment of the possible intricate, indirect, or devious relations between them. Analogical thinking implies ignorance of the lines of demarcation between different concepts, and is therefore facile and delusive. It is valid, if ever, only by accident. When analogical thinking is the method of choice in medicine, clinical validation, where attempted at all, is based solely on anecdote.

Those physicians who shrug off a suffering patient because

they regard his condition as psychosomatic or hypochondriacal are not acting as professional healers, even though they do so either on account of the economic problems created by the time-consuming nature of treating these conditions or because of the frustration stemming from their inability to help. By virtue of being professional healers their only choice ought to be to strive to address themselves to the core of the illness—be it artificially categorized as mental, physical, psychosomatic, or hypochondriacal—and that core is the patient's anguish.

II. HYPOCHONDRIA TODAY:
A Close Look

*I have always felt the obscurity
in the question of hypochondria
to be a disgraceful gap in our
work.*

—*Freud*

Martin S. is a middle-aged salesman who lives in a New York suburb with his family. It's an ordinary morning for him: he has taken a laxative, a couple of pills for his allergies, and breakfasted on prune juice. He now straps on his back brace, takes the first five-milligram Valium of the day, and sets off for work. A good many doctors have told Martin S. that he is not allergic to anything clinically detectable, that his digestion is sound, and that a series of expensive X rays revealed nothing unusual about his back. Martin S. is a hypochondriac.

The following entries have been excerpted from a diary kept by a thirty-five-year-old hypochondriacal CPA at the request of his psychiatrist:

> Wonder why I have been so bloated and full all evening since eating dinner (2 pieces of bread and butter, 1 cup of cocoa). Food seems to stay in my stomach. I know I shall never be my normal self.
>
> Saturday: Cut lawn. So easily tired that must rest every 10 minutes. As usual, also bothered with indigestion. Had eruptions on stomach and back.

Sunday: Panicky at breakfast. A fear is always with me. I must have very little blood the way cold affects me. My hands are numb for an hour or more.

Tuesday: Getting thoroughly disgusted. Severe pain in left shoulder. Saw doctor. Had shoulder and side bound with elastic tape, but no relief.

Thursday: Removed tape; my back covered with large red pimples.

Tuesday: Diet has come down to bread and milk, except for an orange and an egg for breakfast. More nervous each day.

Friday: Severe gas pains in stomach. Ate nothing, drank a quart of cocoa.

Sunday: In addition to being upset, have had what felt like bristles in my throat. It seems I shall never be relieved.

Wednesday: Terrible pains in lower stomach. Had injection from another doctor.

Thursday: Quit drinking cocoa. Believe it may upset me. Refuse to eat any of the following: Coffee, tea, cocoa, pepper, sauces, beer, meat, fish, vegetables, nuts, fruits, pastries, etc.

The composer of this sad diary was referred to a psychiatrist by his family physician whose extensive and repeated examinations, laboratory tests, and X rays had found nothing clinically wrong with him. Psychiatric referral became inevitable when the patient became emaciated and dangerously weakened by his self-imposed diet.

"Got up in sad hypochondria," wrote James Boswell in his journal one day in 1777. "Was quite in despair. Could not see any good purpose in human life. . . . Sunk into dreadful melancholy, so that I went out to the wood and groaned."

Francine Du Plessix Gray reminisced about her hypochondriacal governess in the following words:

She suffered from migraine, constipation, chronic bronchitis, piles, fallen arches, ingrown toenails, eye infections, slipped discs. . . . The closet of my room was turned, overnight, into an apothecary shop filled with phials of ointments, unguents, salves, emetics, and vermifuges; with clysters, enema bags, poultices,

icebags, and hot water bottles; with paper bags, labeled in her fine
slanting hand, containing unbleached wheat germ, fresh yoghurt
culture, linden, mint, camomile, dried verbena . . .

Hypochondriacal symptoms are exceedingly common: they occur
alone or with other symptoms, in mild and severe, acute and
chronic disturbances. It has been conservatively estimated in an
editorial in the *American Journal of Psychotherapy* that more
than 50 percent of all patients seen by physicians in the United
States suffer from such symptoms, and the *Wall Street Journal*
has claimed that hypochondriacs may consume as much as 20
percent of the multibillion-dollar U.S. health budget. By any
estimate, hypochondriacs in the United States alone number in
the millions.

Nevertheless, despite the prevalence of hypochondria, the
illness has been neglected as a subject of medical or psychological
interest for approximately the past hundred years. A review of
the relatively meager literature during that period reveals that
there is no agreement among authorities on *any single aspect* of
hypochondria, both in the medical and psychological disciplines.
Moreover, the majority of physicians of all specialties take a dim
view of hypochondria as a condition and of individuals who suffer
from it. They feel that seeing hypochondriacal patients is a waste
of time and they do so only out of economic or humanitarian
considerations. With few exceptions, they are unwilling to accept
hypochondria as a condition that lends itself to conventional
medical treatment and prefer to regard the obvious and genuine
suffering of hypochondriacs either as an imaginary or psychological problem. Unfortunately, when one looks for psychological
answers, one finds only confusion and disagreement.

This situation is aggravated by the fact that those few who
study, write about, and classify hypochondriacs base their
findings only on the patients they see at their offices and hospitals. It is, however, indisputable—as it emerged during the preparation of this book—that a great many, perhaps even the majority
of, hypochondriacs are "in the closet." They almost never go to

doctors, they do not discuss their condition with casual acquaintances or even their families, and they reveal their sufferings only to a few trusted friends.

The prevailing negative attitudes toward hypochondria are largely unexplained, unjustified, and certainly unjust to victims of the condition. Moreover, they are beclouded by the mystery of why it should be so, when sufferers from anorexia, depression, schizophrenia, and other "nervous" and "mental" states are being offered the rich resources of all specialties of medicine, and their condition bears neither stigma nor ridicule. Hypochondria has become a sort of aesthetic leprosy, and hypochondriacs are at best patronized and belittled and at worst dismissed and ignored—there being only a sparsely inhabited area between the extreme positions. Meanwhile, hypochondriacs themselves are as bewildered and confused as is the majority of the medical community; lacking medical and psychological help, they are preoccupied not only with their bodies, but also with the idea that they are hypochondriacs, devising countless theories to explain themselves to themselves.

How did hypochondria come to be relegated to its present position of neglect in medicine and psychology after many centuries of keen scholarly and popular interest?

The first notions concerning hypochondria were formulated by the Hippocratic and later Greek schools, invested with the authority of Galen, and they remained essentially unchallenged until the seventeenth century. The condition was attributed to disturbances in the soft parts of the body below the rib cage—which is the nearly literal translation of the Greek term transcribed as *hypo-chondros*. The Latinized singular form, *hypochondrium*, connoted the viscera situated in the *hypochondria*, that is, the liver, gallbladder, and spleen. Culpepper, an English physician, among many others, wrote in 1652 of "the liver, gall-bladder and spleen, and the diseases that arise from them, as the jaundice and the hypochondria." By a misapprehension that *hypochondria* was a feminine substantive singular, and by a transfer of meaning, the term came to be used for the condition itself.

The condition came to be increasingly regarded as equivalent in men to hysteria in women—"hysteria" deriving from .the Greek *hystera,* meaning "uterus." Writing in the second century, Aretaeus epitomized the view which was to hold currency for the following fifteen hundred years:

> In the middle of the flanks of women lies the womb, a female viscus, closely resembling an animal: for it is moved of itself hither and thither in the flanks, also upward in a direct line . . . and also obliquely to the right and left . . . in a word it is altogether erratic. It delights also in fragrant smells and advances towards them; and it has an aversion to fetid smells, and flees from them.

Large sections of medieval and Renaissance pharmacopoeias were devoted to various concoctions to be applied at one or another orifice to attract or drive the wandering *hystera* back to its proper place.

As late as the seventeenth century, Thomas Sydenham had no doubt about the equivalence of hysteria and hypochondria. Hysteria occurred "in such male subjects as lead a sedentary or studious life and grow pale over their books and papers . . . However much antiquity may have laid the blame of hysteria upon the uterus, hypochrondria is as like it as one egg is to another." In the early 1700s, Richard Blackmore remarked that "the symptoms that disturb the operations of the mind and imagination in hysterick women, are the same with those in hypochondriacal men, with some inconsiderable variety."

Ernst von Feuchtersleben, the nineteenth-century psychiatrist, who coined the term "psychosis," was unambiguous: "Hysteria, the sister condition of hypochondria, whatever nice distinctions may be between them, is only the same disturbance of the general well-being of the body as modified in the female sex." Yet despite all the evidence to the contrary, Freud appears to have thought that Charcot had "discovered" hysteria in men, and following Charcot, elevated hysteria to a special diagnostic entity, separating it from its centuries-old association with hypochondria.

Galen's pathology of hypochondria, after fifteen hundred years of variation on the basic theme, culminated by the seventeenth century in that refinement of the system of "humours" which attributed the condition to disorders of the spleen, the vapors, and perturbations of the animal spirits. Robert Burton, whose famous *Anatomy of Melancholy* remains a monument to his own hypochondria, quotes ancient and medieval authors in the Galenic tradition, but pronounces: "Most commonly fear, grief, and some sudden commotion or perturbations of the mind begin it, in such bodies especially as are ill disposed." Burton was well ahead of his time in this view, for it wasn't for another hundred years and more that the belief that hypochondria was a mental or nervous disorder began to gain ground. The point was still being argued in the early nineteenth century, but the question was generally considered decided by Jean-Pierre Falret's *De Phypocondrie et du suicide.*

Over the same centuries, many writers have remarked that preoccupation with and concern over the functions of the body and mind—in other words, hypochondria—regularly, if not invariably, precede and accompany severe mental illness. As Nicholas Robinson observed in 1739:

> Madness and lunacy are only the spleen and vapours improved, in different constitution . . . It necessarily follows that they must arise from the same causes, more highly advanced into the habit, which render all the symptoms more dejecting in the melancholy madness, and the more bold, furious and violent in lunacy or the maniacal madness.

By the middle of the nineteenth century, Wilhelm Griesinger was able to say that

> the hypochondriacal states represent the mildest, most moderate form of insanity. While they share with the others the general character of dejection, sadness, depression of mind, diminution of

the activity of the will and a delirium which corresponds to this mental disposition, they yet differ from them in this characteristic manner—that in these states the emotional depression proceeds from a strong feeling of bodily illness which constantly keeps the attention of the patient concentrated upon itself. . . .

These samplings from the literature prior to the arrival of psychoanalysis denote not only the extent of interest in hypochondria, but also a probing yet sympathetic approach. Psychoanalytic formulations brought both to an end.

The neglect of hypochondria began with Emil Kraepelin's grouping together of all psychotic conditions in the two main divisions of dementia praecox and manic-depressive insanity and his view of hypochondria as a symptom of many mental illnesses, and the subsequent revision of this concept by Swiss psychiatrist Eugen Bleuler under the influence of psychoanalytic ideas. But more important to the gradual neglect of hypochondria was the influence of psychoanalytic theory which generally held the belief that chronic or severe hypochondria represented a variety of schizophrenia, while its milder forms were equivalent to anxiety states. In his original monograph on schizophrenia, Bleuler baldly stated that "most incurable hypochondriacs are schizophrenics whose delusions are primarily concerned with their own bodies." Later, he came to regard hypochondria as a personality trait rather than a medical entity: "We no longer recognize hypochondria as a disease."

Freud did much to add to the growing confusion over and diminishing interest in hypochondria, and his uncertainties about the problem seem to have inhibited his followers from generating original ideas. His chief contribution to the subject of body complaint was his definition and discussion of the anxiety state with its symptoms of palpitations, choking, and so forth, which he considered to be ultimately due to reflex irritability from the sexual organs. He says that hypochondria is the form favored by true neurasthenics when they fall victim to the anxiety neurosis.

Neurasthenia—always an ill-defined term—is, according to Freud, a physical exhaustion of the nerve cells—a curiously biophysical notion. Cases of masturbation conflict with bodily complaint were classified by Freud as neurasthenics, thus adding to the masturbation lore. Hypochondria, like neurasthenia, is in fact classified by Freud among the "actual neuroses," as opposed to the psychoneuroses, implying an organic basis—specifically, an increased blood supply to the site of the body complaint of hypochondria, resulting from dammed-up libido.

In his analysis of Dr. Schreber, a paranoid patient who had various bodily complaints, such as TB and softening of the brain, Freud proceeded at once to the psychic mechanisms, which he regarded as castration desires, and quite ignored any analysis of the hypochondria.

Paul Schilder considered hypochondria as a type of narcissism—"increased self-love, but self-love turned in such a way that the individual defends himself against his own self-love." Adler made no particular contribution to the problem. He regarded hypochondria as a part of the inferiority complex and in special relation to the organic inferiority.

Sandor Ferenczi had a keen interest in hypochondria and he was probably the first to call Freud's attention to it. In one place he speaks of hypochondria resulting from a genital inferiority. But, in a later paper, he feels convinced that "in many cases hypochondria is really a fermentative product of anal erotism, a displacement of unsublimated coprophilic interests from their original objects on to other organs and products of the body with an alteration of the qualifying pleasure"—a yeasty metaphor of the art of brewery. The choice of the organ toward which the hypochondria is directed is determined by special factors, such as "somatic disposition."

The orthodox psychoanalytic position stresses three factors as having importance in the evolvement of hypochondria: libidinal frustration, narcissistic withdrawal, and guilt feelings. This means that when satisfaction cannot be gained from the usual libidinal objects in the environment, the individual reinvests the libido in himself. This results in a hypernarcissistic state in which the prominence and importance of one's own body are intensified. At the same time, since the impulses withdrawn from external objects are to some degree always hostile and sadistic, they represent, when turned back upon the self, a form of self-attack. They cause pain and suffering, but may also serve as an important guilt-relieving function. From this point of view, hypochondria is a state of magnified narcissism which is a reaction to frustration, and also a form of self-attack which relieves guilt. Alexander summarized this view in the following passage:

> When frustrated in their demands for admiration by others, they themselves give their bodies all the attention they previously received. Frustration also mobilizes competitive hostile impulses which have been dormant as long as they received love and attention. These hostile impulses revive earlier competitive conflicts of family life, such as oedipal guilt, and sibling rivalry. This guilt creates a need for suffering. The hypochondriacal symptom satisfies both needs; the patient gives love and attention to his own body and at the same time relieves guilt by suffering.

Related analytic positions have been expressed by many others with minor variations and varying emphases, such as Otto Fenichel's view of the hypochondriacal anxiety as representing castration anxiety, and Karen Horney's insistence on the importance of the self-punishing aspects of the hypochondriacal experience. On the whole, however, the psychoanalytic contribution to the subject has a forced quality to it, with each writer seemingly straining to fit hypochondria into his schema, yet not managing to take it quite seriously. Differences in terminology and psychodynamic formulations bedevil much of this area, and such terms as "organ neurosis," "erotization of organs," "vegetative neurosis," "somatoneurosis," and "pathoneurosis" do little to clarify the situation.

One interesting exception is worth noting. John L. Cameron, a psychiatrist, sketched a psychologically and existentially acute view that differs from the usual analytic formulations. He portrayed hypochondria primarily as a means for displacing one's general inadequacy from oneself to one's body. It presumably provides a means for avoiding responsibility and denying failure. Cameron also suggested that it could be utilized to control others—to manipulate them into acceding to one's expectations and demands. Further, he cites instances in which it may serve paradoxically as a way for an individual to integrate and focus his energies. Body preoccupation can become a distorted vehicle for channeled self-expression. The hypochondriacal individual is using his body to express conflicts and to mobilize interest and help from others, to symbolize his sense of vulnerability in a threatening world, and to experience life mainly through his body.

Ida Macalpine and Richard A. Hunter noted that patients with hypochondriacal tendencies present an infinite variety of clinical pictures, and they suggest that it is convenient to distinguish four stages of severity. In the earliest, the patient may complain only of abdominal symptoms—indigestion, nausea, constipation, and so on—and appear to all intents and purposes mentally normal. Other patients may not volunteer any body symptoms at this stage at all, unless specifically asked, and may complain only of anxiety, insomnia, inability to concentrate, and other symptoms of depression.

In the second stage, patients tend to localize their altered sensation more precisely. They speak of feeling "as if" something were stuck in their throat, or moving about in their stomach, or crawling on or under their skin.

After a time, some patients may pass into the third stage, while others may remain settled into the second. Those in the third stage now take their altered sensations more seriously and "as if" becomes a certainty. No longer concerned that they may develop a certain disease, they are now convinced that they have it. At this stage, no longer amenable to reassurance and objective evidence of lack of pathology, patients begin to go from doctor to doctor in quest of confirmation of their delusions. They become irritable, suspicious, feel aggrieved, wronged, or persecuted, and may misinterpret what they are being told or even what is happening to them.

For some, this stage may pass imperceptibly into the fourth, when delusions no longer remain confined to the body, but become related to the outside world. These patients now develop ideas of reference and influence, ascribing their altered body sensations to external agencies—poison, rays, the CIA, and so on. Such individuals are now patently paranoiac, alienated from external reality.

This process is not restricted to body sensations; many mental symptoms can also be understood in terms of the patient's altered relation to his mind. Burton, over three hundred years ago, recognized the essential similarity of "the hypochondriacal or windy melancholy" to what he called "head-melancholy." Patients complain that they cannot think properly, cannot concentrate or remember, that they are obsessed by recurring thoughts or ideas, or have compulsively to perform certain acts. They may fear that their brain "may snap," or that they will lose control of their nerves or mind.

Macalpine and Hunter emphasize that they are not propounding a general theory, and they prefer not to use psychoanalytic terms with all their implied assumptions as to the structure of the mental apparatus. But they hold that hypochondria is not explicable either as the outcome of maladaptation to environment, or as neurotic resolution of conflict through the use of mental mechanisms.

They believe that the first-stage symptoms can be traced to a recent stimulus provided by reality, the significance of which is not consciously apparent to the patient. This leads to the activation of normally unconscious fantasies and associated emotions, which achieve disguised body expression in the specific symptom. But, the emotion achieves only partial expression in the symptom, so that instead of leading to some action and thus subsiding, it persists in the guise of the symptom. The symptom is therefore not a defense mechanism of the mature mind, but a more primitive phenomenon, concerned with beliefs, wishes, and fears relating to the functioning and structure of the body and mind. This theory smacks unmistakably of the psychoanalytic terms Macalpine and Hunter disdain, and it is perplexing to try to separate it from the theory of neurotic resolution of conflict, which they renounce.

Scrutiny of the psychoanalytic literature, aided by the examination of hundreds of case histories of hypochondriacs as well as by interviews with scores of hypochondriacs, enables one to attempt a concise condensation of the sensible parts of psychoanalytic theories:

It is a prime axiom in psychological medicine that the symptom that is consciously not desired by the patient and that he thinks of as his problem may be unconsciously the solution to his problem. Common sense tells us that the symptom formation of hypochondria subserves a set of hidden needs and purposes that are no less genuine for being unconscious. Perhaps the foremost unconscious need subserved by all hypochondriacal suffering is the assuagement of a conviction of guilt. Not invariably, but usually, the guilt has been unconsciously repressed and is not available to conscious awareness.

It is also axiomatic that unconscious, or irrational, guilt can be produced by a series of mechanisms. One is related to the fact that the infantile mind is unable to differentiate between thinking and doing. It holds itself equally culpable for the thought and the deed. For example, if a parent or sibling dies, the child unconsciously believes that his "evil thoughts" or death wishes caused the death, and that he is therefore responsible for it as the murderer. He feels guilt, and, because guilt is so painful and unacceptable, it is more or less quickly repressed from awareness. It does not, however, cease to exist, but continues to motivate a need for expiation.

Another principle is the "law of talion," a concept that holds that guilt of a crime, actual or fantasied, can be assuaged or alleviated only by an identical or very similar punishment. In the above example, the child may become frightened, fearful, and develop symptoms similar or identical to those of the loved person who died. This accounts for the reluctance of the hypochondriac to surrender his physical symptoms, for if he unconsciously believes that as long as he suffers he is protected

from a more dreaded punishment, then it would be not only a bad
bargain but a positive danger to get well. The powers that be will
not destroy us as long as we punish ourselves—an atavistic belief
of mankind, expressed in many religions in the form of sacrifice to
the gods, or the concept of "hubris" in the ancient Greek
religion. Nothing terrifies the hypochondriac as much as to be
well. Paradoxical as it may seem, illness staves off the possibility
of death, because illness is suffering. This protective value of
illness is very frequently present in the psychodynamics of the
hypochondriac.

An additional factor is the employment of illness as a physical expression of an associated sense of lack of inner worth, a
deficit of self-esteem. As the case histories will demonstrate,
hypochondriacs not only have histories of relationships studded
with hostile ambivalence to parental figures, but these figures
themselves were usually damaged physiologically or psychologically. Also, hypochondriacs were usually raised in an atmosphere
of illness by persons who have made much of illness and physical
complaints, and we know that it is unconsciously hard for a child
to feel stronger and more adequate than they perceive the parents
to be. Feelings of self-esteem in childhood are developed magi-
cally, not logically, and the child perceives himself as his parents
perceive him to be, and thus grows up thinking of his body as a
damaged, frail mechanism, not equal to life's tasks. Mary I.
Preston's pioneering study of hypochondria in children noted that
in the majority of her patients distressing and often intolerable
situations were discovered. Symptoms corroborating serious
trouble were found to be excessive daydreaming, crying and
going to pieces easily, being worried and anxious much of the
time, playing alone, and, in the case of children of above-average
intelligence, a decreased learning ability. In over 95 percent of her
cases, physical complaints were found to serve a definite and
important need in the children's lives, that of ameliorating intolerable situations or of solving intricate problems beyond their
powers. Perpetuation of these complaints led to hypochondria
and other disorders in 80 percent of cases.

A number of writers agree that changes in body image can lead to pathological self-observation and delusions described by French psychiatrists as *"délire métabolique,"* or *"délire de métamorphose."* Furthermore, the concept of body image has become the starting point of a psychoanalytic doctrine of hypochondria, in which an increased libidinous fixation on organs and parts of the body accounts for the hypochondriacal preoccupation.

The body image plays a specific part in hypochondriacal states in which a discongruity is experienced by the patient between the body image and the laws of gravity, which leads to continual self-observation. A German psychiatrist describes the case of a man who performed constant acrobatics with the utmost persistence, in order to put right the position of his head which he believed to be turned around the wrong way.

The best sources of material about body-image phenomena come from reports of neurotic and psychotic patients, due to the dramatic alterations of body feeling that often accompany personality disorganization. Josef Breuer and Freud were among the first to devote systematic attention to the symbolic values that may be ascribed to various body areas and to point out that these values may become vehicles for progressing psychopathology. In their work with conversion hysterics, for example, they arrived at the formulation that the body part rendered nonfunctional by a conversion symptom is typically one to which unconscious sexual significance had been assigned, and the incapacitation of the part represents an attempt to block the expression of sexual wishes.

Since this early work, the relationship between body image and personality pathology has received the attention of a long line of successors of Freud and Breuer. Seymour Fisher has summarized the body-image questions they had raised as being of the following order:

1. Is body image important in the process of ego formation, and, if so, what kinds of body-image deficiencies are most likely to produce ego instability?

2. What conditions affect the developing individual's ability to establish firm body-image boundaries, and how significant is this for later maturity?
3. How do body-image attitudes affect the translation of repressed fantasies into body sensations and body dysfunctions?
4. What body-image factors may produce disturbance in the individual's ability to adopt a consistent sex role and to be sexually expressive?
5. Under conditions of severe regression, how do body-image distortions influence misinterpretations of the outside world?

As one reviews pertinent psychoanalytic publications of recent years, it is apparent that they continue to be concerned with the same fundamental questions.

Felix Deutsch has, in the original Freudian tradition, maintained a long-standing interest in conversion hysteria. He developed a rather elaborate theory to show how the individual attaches symbolic meanings to his body. He suggests that the newborn child recognizes the existence of his own body only. Everything he perceives seems to be a part of him. However, he soon discovers that what he considers to be part of himself (chiefly, mother) can be lost for varying periods of time. What he thinks is part of his body disappears, and he is left with a sense of body loss. According to Deutsch, this results in persistent wishes to restore the body's losses by regaining body possession of important outside objects. Conversion occurs when at some point the individual suffers an object loss which is so serious that he has to "retroject" in fantasy important substitute objects. Presumably, in the course of such retrojection, body sensations and body events originally associated with the retrojected object may be aroused and result in pathological physiological disturbances, labeled as conversion symptoms.

Thomas Szasz views the hysterical symptom as an "iconic sign," a mode of communication between sufferer and another person. He believes that the individual is particularly likely to use his body as a means for communicating what cannot be transmitted by other means. Szasz depicts many varieties of body complaints, sensations, and pains as primarily serving communication functions.

Phyllis Greenacre devoted a good deal of attention to body-image factors underlying behavioral disturbance. She speculated on the basis of her clinical work that early body experiences, body rhythms, and modes of body exploration are basic to the individual's sense of identity. She proposes that an individual's images of his face and genitals are especially fundamental to his body scheme, and that distortions in these images enhance vulnerability to later disturbances. She cites the difficulties encountered by a young woman, who had a congenital absence of vaginal opening, in establishing a meaningful body image and identity. So disturbed was this attractive woman about her image that she developed a severe phobia of mirrors.

In the same vein, Keiser attributes difficulties in learning and abstract reasoning to body-image distortions. He reports that in several patients who had severe problems in learning and abstracting, there was an unusual lack of knowledge, even denial, of body openings, particularly the vagina and anus. He makes the farfetched point that these orifices are not easily available for visual inspection, and their existence must, therefore, be logically deduced. Hence, these patients have learning and abstracting dysfunctions.

It is evident even from this brief sampling that body-image factors have been seriously implicated in a great variety of behavioral phenomena, including, of course, hypochondria. It is difficult to think of an area of behavior that has not been scanned within the context of the possible influence of the body image. There is a disconcerting range of ideas about the nature of body image, and much disagreement on which of its aspects are worthy of study. For some researchers, body image is largely what a subject is willing to tell them when he is asked how he feels about his body—and it is these writers who make the most of the role of body image in hypochondria. For others, the body image is a more cryptic phenomenon whose measurement requires devious strategies.

From the point of view of hypochondria, the most relevant area of body-image studies is the one that concerns itself with how positively or negatively the individual regards his body. Such body evaluations typically involve stating how satisfied one is with the appearance of a number of different areas of his body. They relate to the basic question of whether the individual likes or dislikes his body. While few would question that whether a person is satisfied with the attractiveness of his body represents an important facet of how he experiences it, there is no agreement on how to measure this factor. All sorts of self-report and scale methods of measurements have been devised for this purpose, but there is no consensus on their respective effectiveness.

The perception of one's body size is another relevant issue. The accumulated data indicate that when an individual judges the size of a part of his body, he is influenced by factors other than the real size of the part, chiefly, his emotional attitudes about himself and his body. His perception of his bodily size may reflect his level of self-esteem, or his need to prove his superiority to women. Sensations of change in body-size perception often accompany special emotional events. Experiences of full-blown body-size change have been described in relation not only to hypochondria, but to schizophrenic regression, migraine attacks, transference attitudes during psychoanalytic therapy, and brain damage. Major shifts in the individual's adjustment level seem to be translated into alterations in perceived body size.

Occasional clues in the body-image literature indicate that people differ in how aware they are of their bodies as compared to the world around them. Some have very high awareness of the body, others are only minimally aware of it; the fact that extremes of body awareness can occur is exemplified in the hypochondriacal individual who is completely preoccupied with it. There is a wide variation in the number of body associations given to the stimulus words in the Secord Homonym Test, which was devised to measure how concerned the individual is about his body by counting how often he gives body versus nonbody associations to homonyms that have both body and nonbody meaning, for example, "colon." It is pertinent to note that in some disorganized states, such as schizophrenia or brain damage, marked tendencies may appear to be either totally focused on one's body or to ignore it, even to the extent of denying its existence.

Another point to consider with reference to hypochondria and body awareness is how a person distributes his attention to the major sectors of his body. One finds abundant examples in which a specific body area becomes the focus for hypochondriacal concern, or delusional ideas and sensations, while persons asking for cosmetic surgery certainly display special awareness of a body region. It has been reported that people vary in valuations they place on body areas when asked to judge their worth and importance, and that they display idiosyncratic reactions when evaluating the masculinity and femininity of specific body areas.

Anxiety about the body is another relevant point. Some people are apparently chronically afraid of body damage, while others are quite unconcerned about the possibility. The existence of this factor was first proposed by Freud and other psychoanalysts in their studies dealing with "castration anxiety." Fear of body damage is dramatically highlighted in the behavior of the hypochondriac and is similarly apparent in the patient awaiting surgery. Interestingly, body damage is a frequent theme in children's stories and in dreams. Little or no information is available on how body anxiety is related to other kinds of anxiety. A mature adult can fear all kinds of things in the world without seriously anticipating body damage. On the other hand, a hypochondriac may be consumed with body anxiety and be completely oblivious to other anxieties.

It has been shown that men seek to dramatize the bigness of their bodies, while women the smallness of theirs. In a related vein, men are more likely than women to convert feelings of failure into sensations of diminished height. Women tend to shrink and men to augment the extent of most of their body proportions. Also, it has been reported that women are more

dissatisfied than men with the lower areas of their bodies, indicating that the sexes have different degrees of difficulty or
anxiety in evaluating upper- versus lower-body sectors. After age
thirteen, males clearly place less emphasis on the body than do
females; the latter have been found to be higher in body concern
on the Secord Homonym Test.

G. A. Ladee describes a long array of past speculations about
the role of body image in hypochondriacal behavior, and, as a
rule, they are generally vague and rarely presented in testable
form. Illustratively, there are assertions that the hypochondriac is
using his body to express conflicts and to arouse interest and
sympathy from others, to symbolize his sense of vulnerability in a
threatening world, to experience life only through his body.

Clearly, body-image studies contain a great deal of material
relevant to hypochondria and hypochondriacs, but the material is
no less diffuse, no less contradictory, than that of psychoanalytic
or psychiatric investigations of the subject. Without meaning to
put the onus for this state of affairs on one profession, it is
entirely possible that psychiatry has obviously not yet reached
the stage where it can delineate, in Karl Jaspers's words,

> genuine natural disease entities which have similar causes, a similar
> basic psychological form, similar development and course, similar
> outcome, and a similar cerebral pathology and which, therefore, all
> present the same over-all picture.

What does medical literature have to say on the subject of
common personality traits of hypochondriacs? The most frequently observed trait is concentration on bodily sensations that
are used to substantiate another equally frequent trait, namely,
the conviction of having a well-established disease. It is also a
matter of general observation that hypochondriacs are more than
ordinarily suggestible. They are particularly easy prey to pessimistic suggestions regarding illnesses, which they receive from
all available sources. This accounts in part for the great variety of
hypochondriacal complaints and for the easy shifting of the
hypochondriac's attention from one organ to another, and from

one disease to another—a trait many doctors frivolously refer to as the "organ recital."

Other personality traits pointed out are egocentricity, pride of a defiant nature, miserliness, reliability, conscientiousness in performing petty duties, obstinacy that may grow into defiance, irascibility, vindictiveness, distrust, hatred of the world, tendency to accuse others. Freud recognized three fundamental character traits: orderliness, parsimoniousness, obstinacy. Orderliness includes excessive cleanliness, reliability, over-conscientiousness; obstinacy is associated with irascibility and vindictiveness. The conspicuous absence of tender, humane traits from these observations makes one wonder how so many hypochondriacs manage to acquire and hold on to friends, lovers, careers, even success and relative serenity.

In certain writings less emphasis is placed on individual personality traits. What is pointed to as the essential characteristic of the hypochondriac is his very special personality makeup, characterized by an excessive, morbid preoccupation with health, although his mental functioning remains otherwise unimpaired. One writer speaks of "constitutional hypochondria" in which the unhealthy attitude toward health and illness manifests itself from early childhood and progresses with age. This morbid predisposition is placed in the group of "constitutional psychopathies."

Granting the existence of a certain predisposition to hypochondria, two sets of environmental factors are regarded as likely to provoke it. The first comprises personal experiences of hypochondriacs with others in the routine of their daily activities, feelings of inadequacy and desire to escape worldly responsibilities, thwarted ambitions, petty jealousies, retirement without hobbies or interests, temporary but long periods of idleness, convalescence, and forced unemployment. In addition the doctor's attitude in his relationship with the patient, incautious remarks, thinking out loud in the patient's presence, and obviously unwise medical management of individuals who are essentially predisposed to collect diseases are all held greatly responsible for the so-called iatrogenic (physician-caused) hypochondrias.

The second set of environmental factors do not directly involve either the personal relationships of the hypochondriac or his habitual mode of living, yet they prove to be potent contributing agents in provoking and maintaining hypochondriacal states. They include opinions and advice picked up from friends and acquaintances, popular medical literature, advertisements of spectacularly beneficial effects of drugs in specific diseases, and government- and foundation-sponsored health propaganda disseminated by the media. This type of information has only a moderate, if any, influence on the nonhypochondriac but can provoke disease-consciousness in the hypochondriacally predisposed. The late French writer Jules Romains, who was a physician, portrays in his comedy, *Doctor Knock,* the rendering of a whole community disease-conscious by an enterprising physician. Following his professional philosophy, that it is the physician's job to get as many patients as possible, Dr. Knock does indeed succeed in causing the entire community to become afflicted with hypochondriacal disorders.

Clearly, there is no agreement on what constitutes the hypochondriacal personality. Even the qualities that occur most frequently, that is, conscientiousness, obstinacy, frugality, but also sensitivity, shyness, sociability—all of which are regarded as anal traits—even these can be clearly shown in only 25 percent to a maximum of 40 percent of cases.

There is however, one common denominator of the hypochondriacal personality that has been noted almost without exception by investigators: *Hypochondriacs are highly unsure of themselves, despite a sometimes open, but usually carefully hidden, assertiveness, and they live in a striking dependence relationship to a parent or a parent substitute.* Among men, this is usually the mother, toward whom a slavish submissiveness continues to exist or against whom there is powerless rebellion; less frequently, it is fear and admiration of the father. In numerous cases, there is a factor of extreme spoiling and/or overanxious protection by the mother, who may nevertheless be lacking in warmth. Men are fairly often either the youngest or the only son, or a combination of the two, but rather seldom an only child.

In many cases, such an upbringing had been aggravated by the presence of ill health in the family. Excessive maternal anxiety is often connected by children with an excessive interest in the body, and so are illnesses of loved ones in the family, frequent contact with hospitals, doctors, or stress on bodily cleanliness and hygiene. There is a strong identification with the mother who is insistent on the care of the body, and also with the overanxious mother who frequently talks about how difficult it was to deliver the child and stresses the danger it posed to her own life.

Passive-tyrannical fathers are a common finding; they are nonmasculine, doubt-ridden, inhibited and inhibiting of the activities of the family, always on the defensive against emotional and aggressive wives, always tending to enlist as allies doctors and specialists of all sorts.

Among female hypochondriacs, spoiling, especially by the father, is equally common; the father whose favorite they were is likely to have been strict and subject to fits of rage, and they, unlike his other children, could get to do anything. A strong bond with a pampering mother is rare among women.

It is noticeable that the throat is a preferred organ of hypochondriacal symptoms in this group. One patient, a twenty-five-year-old man, felt his throat to be so tormenting that he "could never be himself"; his body became his enemy and persecutor. He felt betrayed, hurt, and blamed his condition on his mother. He manipulated his throat so aggressively that violent hemorrhages occurred, almost resulting in self-multilation.

There is a widespread false belief that hypochondria is rooted in weak intellectual judgment and that there is an affinity for feeblemindedness. It may be true that with prolonged and repeated contact with hypochondriacs one is struck by their monotonous, rigid way of life, but they are certainly not feeble-minded. Their frustrated aggression, coupled with self-curtailed creativity, often leads to an underestimation by others of their capabilities, so that their social level is often lower than their potential for attaining a higher level of accomplishment. By and large, the intellectual and educational levels of hypochondriacs are certainly above the average.

Hypochondria is seldom mentioned in connection with brilliant and creative figures. Hypochondriacs generally feel that it is an exercise in futility to recite lists of their famous brethren, among them, Burton, Swift, Samuel Johnson, Boswell, Molière, Voltaire, the Goncourt brothers, who had hypochondriacal concern for each other, Gide, Beethoven, and Kant. They all struggled valiantly against hypochondria with an enormous display of creative activity. Their attitude has been accurately put by Dr. Johnson in a letter to the complaining Boswell:

> You are always complaining of melancholy, and I conclude from those complaints that you are fond of it. No man talks of that which he is desirous to conceal, and every man desires to conceal that of which he is ashamed. Do not pretend to deny it; make it an invariable and obligatory law to yourself, never to mention your own mental diseases; if you are never to speak of them you will think on them but little, and if you think little of them, they will molest you rarely. When you talk of them, it is plain that you want either praise or pity; for praise there is no room, and pity will do you no good; therefore, from this hour speak no more, think no more, about them.

Hereditary disposition to hypochondria was hotly debated around the turn of the twentieth century, and it is still by no means a dead issue, although the term is used in a wider sense today. French psychiatry, in particular, has shown great interest in the subject.

Delmas, writing in the early 1930s, even speaks of a "paranoid constitution"; to him, hypochondria is but a syndrome rooted in the paranoiac condition. Jean Abadie, on the other hand, assumes a specific hypochondriac constitution, which he calls *"constitution arganique,"* named after Argan, the principal character in Molière's *The Imaginary Invalid.* His theory is based on a congenital supersensitivity coupled with an anxious, emotional attitude to life.

In fact, there has never been a positive indication of a hereditary disposition to hypochondria. The indisputable existence of many second- even third-generation hypochondriacs can nearly always be traced to childhood circumstances or early traumas, such as the death of a parent or grandparent, or replacement as the favorite child by the arrival of another.

Internal stress has also been mentioned as a causative factor in hypochondria, with somewhat more justification than hereditary disposition. According to this theory, this type of hypochondria is secondary to an existing neurosis, and it needs only a slight special motive, such as stress, to become activated. Ladee observed, especially in men, patterns of increasing uncertainty in regard to the results of work or study, coupled with sexual uncertainty, fear of impotence, and very often, an activation of guilt and punishment anxiety with regard to masturbation. However, it strikes one as futile to sort out accurately the hypochondriacal content from the neurotic components in these conditions. Internal stress is a complex enough phenomenon, with unpredictable and inconsistent consequences, to need the introduction of hypochondriacal syndromes.

External and somatic stress is often mentioned in the literature as a cause of hypochondria. Provoking factors relating to physical illness are exceedingly common, such as operations, acute infectious diseases—especially, infectious hepatitis—and recurrent or chronic complaints that require enforced rest. Acute loss of blood and cardiac palpitations in adolescents have also been implicated. Interest in these cases is concentrated on uncertain and unverifiable bodily functions, and such experiences often constitute the starting point for hypochondria, and even for delusional developments.

Other causative influences include real or threatened loss of love, pregnancy of one's wife for males, childbirth for females, short-term threatened confrontation in the course of sex life, such as approaching marriage or first coitus, and acute occupational problems, such as being passed over for promotion, or tension before or failure at an examination.

Demographic data relating to hypochondriacs are difficult to come by. The makeup of the "closet" population can only be guessed, which renders the majority unavailable for study; private practitioners have no reason to tabulate such data; hospitals, with strikingly few exceptions, do not treat hypochondria as a disease entity. Consequently, our chief sources of information are published clinical studies, which are—like all other types of information relating to hypochondria—excessively meager. Fewer than ten studies devoted to groups of hypochondriacs have been published in the last fifty years; only one of these was a "controlled" study where a comparison group was used to validate findings, and, unfortunately, even that study failed to employ the criterion of "statistical significance."

F. E. Kenyon, who conducted that study, relied on the case records of 512 hypochondriacal patients attending the Bethlem Royal and Maudsley Hospitals in London over the ten-year period, 1951–60. Although the primary goal was to determine whether there was justification for differentiating between primary and secondary hypochondria, it does contain the most reliable demographic data we have. (Primary hypochondria is in its pure state, unconnected to other illnesses. Secondary hypochondria derives from or is consequent to a primary illness, mental or physical.)

As to *age and sex* incidence, the peak age incidence for males was thirty to thirty-nine, for females, forty to forty-nine, which negates the belief that hypochondria is characteristic of mature age. The factor of *religion* revealed no significant differences, damaging the popular belief that Jews have a higher incidence of hypochondria than members of other religions. There were no differences as to social class or intelligence between the two groups, and the work record of primary hypochondriacs was only slightly inferior to that of the controls. Interestingly, 63 percent of the primary and 68 percent of secondary hypochondriacs were married or cohabiting; only 26 percent of the former and 22 percent of the latter were single.

Classification of physical complaints was done in three different ways: (1) by distribution in different parts of the body, (2) by organic system involved, and (3) whether unilateral or not. The body was divided into eight regions, with two other categories added of "other" and "diffuse." The head and neck were the focus of most complaints by primary as well as secondary hypochondriacs—57 percent and 50 percent, respectively. This was followed in the primary group by the abdomen, other, chest, back, lower limbs, diffuse, anus, upper limbs, and genitalia, with only slight differences in the control group. The three most highly represented regions, head and neck, abdomen, and chest, were in exactly the same order in both.

Analysis of the frequency distribution of complaints by body systems showed that the three most frequently involved were the gastrointestinal, the musculoskeletal, and the central nervous system, the last of which included headaches.

As to laterality, 19 percent of the primary group had definite unilateral symptoms, and of these 65 percent were referred to the left side of the body and 35 percent to the right. While unilaterality stood at only 12 percent in the control group, 81 percent of these were left-sided and 19 percent right-sided. A number of writers seriously suggested that the high proportion of left-sidedness, which had been noted earlier, may be a reflection of the symbolic association of the left with sinister, evil, bad, and irrational; a more probable explanation is the relatively less developed state of the right side of the cerebral hemisphere, which controls the left side of the body.

One of the few findings that seem to be agreed on by the majority of writers is that hypochondria is essentially a male condition, but few attempt any explanation why this should be so. (It is interesting to note that in current U.S. medical literature, the hypochondriacal patient is almost invariably referred to as "she.") Donald Hubble's almost lyrical explanation is that the development of hypochondria requires an immature personality plus environmental overcare, and thinks that it is in the nature of women to bestow this affectionate solicitude, and in the nature of men and children to receive it.

Controlled attempts to investigate other variables underlying hypochondria have been few, despite the fact that the Minnesota Multiphasic Personality Inventory (MMPI), which is one of the most widely used "paper and pencil" tests, contains a Hypochondriasis Scale. This scale was developed by assembling items that would differentiate psychiatric patients with predominantly hypochondriacal complaints from "normals" and neurotics without hypochondriacal complaints. A variety of correlates of the Hypochondriasis Score have been reported, but these are neither consistent nor particularly revealing.

In studying the many attempts that have been made to define and classify hypochondria, one comes across a tremendous variety. F. E. Kenyon collected the following eighteen usages of the term from the medical literature:

Synonymous with madness

A mental disease due to disorders of the digestive tract

A term of abuse in the sense that the hypochondriac is malingering or that all his complaints are imaginary

A general sense of preoccupation with bodily or mental health or functions

A personality trait

A defense mechanism

A neurotic manifestation

An anxiety substitute

An actual neurosis

A manifestation of neurasthenia or depersonalization

The same as hysteria, only in the male

A transitional state between hysteria and psychosis

A disease classification as "primary or essential hypochondriasis"

A symptom of almost any commonly recognized psychiatric syndrome, such as depression or paranoia

An early stage of another illness, for example, schizophrenia

A form of schizophrenia

A disturbance of the sense of normal functioning of the organs of the body (cenesthesiopathy)

A part of a symptomatic psychosis or endogenous reaction

One is further struck by the extraordinary difficulty of arriving at a definition. Even the authors of definitions are seldom satisfied with their formulations. If one starts by defining the concept in very wide terms, using this definition as a basis to arrive at a narrower and more meaningful understanding of the hypochondriacal state, one cannot be too careful in one's choice of the initial concept. For example, if one started from such an obvious definition as that of Oscar Bumke, according to whom hypochondria is *"fear of disease not based on facts,"* one would soon run into trouble. On the one hand, this definition allows so much play that most people who consult a doctor, and many who do not, could be classified as hypochondriacs. On the other hand, the definition excludes all cases where there is no manifest "fear of"; also, the assumption that the fear is not based on facts rests on a dangerous simplification of what we know about the state of illness and health.

Most authors dealing with the subject of hypochondria cannot get away from virtually identical definitions along the lines of fear of disease not based on clinical proof, which is not difficult to understand. The fact is that hypochondriacal patients offer themselves, their bodies, as an object of investigation and discussion. And, apart from the fundamental shortcomings of scientific methods of exploring the human being, even the human body, we must remember that each human being has within himself sources of information that are inaccessible to anyone else. The patient makes ample use of these, so that stating that the fears are "not based on facts" is really a confession of ignorance on the part of the doctor in his attempts to define, diagnose, or treat hypochondria.

Bumke's definition can also lead to a curious paradox. A patient of Wilhelm Jahrreiss (whose invaluable 1930 treatise on hypochondria has yet to be translated into English) was agonized by the fear of being affected by hypochondria. If the patient regards his state as being based on facts, then, according to Bumke, he is ill, not hypochondriacal; if the patient later comes to the conclusion that there is no factual basis for his fears, then we must again conclude that he is not hypochondriacal—a paradox reminiscent of the classic logical paradox of the Cretan stating that all Cretans are liars.

The discussion of various old and new descriptions of hypochondria that follows will show that the more the hypochondriacal patient is viewed in his *entire mode of being,* the better the description, as attempts based on distinguishing "subjective" from "objective" have clearly been fruitless. On these grounds, the two best definitions we have to this day are those of Hans Jolly and Paul Hitzig formulated at the end of the nineteenth century, and R. D. Gillespie's in 1928.

Jolly and Hitzig stated that "hypochondria is that state of anguish ('traurige Verstimmung'), due to a pathological change in self-experience, in which the patient's attention is continually or principally directed towards his own physical or mental state."

Gillespie: "Hypochondria is a mental preoccupation with a real or suppositious physical or mental disorder; a discrepancy between the degree of preoccupation and the grounds for it so that the former is far in excess of what is justified; and an affective condition best characterized as interest with conviction and consequent concern, and with indifference to the opinion of the environment, including irresponsiveness to persuasion."

Gillespie's elegant definition is more comprehensive than most. The word "disorder" allows much more scope than "disease," and more importantly, Gillespie was careful to avoid the terms "fear" and "depression." This view is by no means new; Burton wrote that hypochondriacal melancholy may occur without depression or overt anxiety for "fear and sorrow are not general symptoms: some fear and are not sad; some be sad and fear not, some neither fear nor grieve." Also, Gillespie specifies that the hypochondriac is *preoccupied* excessively; he is not merely interested in his condition, but interested with conviction, which makes him immune to all influences that are contrary to it.

It seems to be true that fear and/or depression are frequently seen in hypochondriacal patients, but as one studies the case histories, it emerges that these states are attached to the clinical picture in the context of which the hypochondria occurs. These are, of course, all cases of secondary hypochondria; nevertheless, many writers, principally psychiatrists, continue to consider fear and depression—the accent being laid sometimes more on fear, sometimes more on depression—as an indispensable characteristic of hypochondria. They do so in spite of the existence of hypochondriacal patients who exhibit no manifest fear or depression, deny any such feelings, or, at most, admit that they are neither cheered nor soothed by their hypochondria. It is very difficult to concede that fear and/or depression are, or should be, considered indispensable to the hypochondriacal state. It is equally very difficult to regard fear of disease in itself as a condition analogous to hypochondria; inevitably and sensibly, *fear of disease properly belongs among the phobias. The phobic person is afraid that he might catch a disease, while the hypochondriac believes that he has already got one.*

When we turn our attention to the ways in which hypochondriacal patients are involved with their preoccupation, again we find no consensus. Some writers on the subject deny that the typical hypochondriacal mode should be characterized by the certainty of the notion of having a certain disease. It is precisely because he is in doubt, because he believes that he is ill but is not yet sure, that the patient rushes from doctor to doctor. Therefore, according to this view, those who are convinced that they are suffering from a particular illness are suffering from a *delusion of disease,* or *somatic delusion.* This would have to be separated from hypochondria, because a paranoid element is much more predominant here.

The mode of the patient's involvement with his preoccupation is the main criterion in Raoul Cardona's definition of hypochondria as "belief with doubt that one has a disease of a serious but not precisely definable nature, which is somewhat accentuated by a positive hope in the efficacy of medical science. This is coupled with a cult regarding the possibility of cure, in which the patient keeps on changing doctors and remedies, and concentrates his entire attention on his body, his complaint, medical literature, and every new drug; he does not blame the doctors for impotence or ignorance, and accepts the fact that the diagnosis cannot be made yet, or that the right medicine has not yet been found.''

This is more or less in tune with Gillespie, except that Gillespie ascribes to the hypochondriac a stronger belief and a much weaker doubt. He, unlike Cardona, denies that there are fear and depression inherent in the specifically hypochondriacal mode.

In order to do justice to the fluctuation between doubt and conviction, which is intrinsically characteristic of most hypochondriacal states, we would do well to follow Jahrreiss's arguments. He sees the hypochondriacal image or idea as the decisive psychopathological component of hypochondria, and this is not comparable to an obsessive or paranoiac idea. Thus, the accent is shifted entirely to the *substance* of the patient's preoccupation. This substance relates to damage, disturbance, change, or disease of the body or mind, which is not founded on objective facts, but which is not an error, only a baseless supposition. In other words, it is a fantasy and thus more difficult to correct than an error, which is merely a false conclusion. In principle—but not in fact—this fantasy can, however, also be corrected, whereas a delusion cannot. Jahrreiss then arrives at the definition that ''the hypochondriac idea is the fantasy of being ill.''

In his arguments, the hypochondriacal idea occupies a central position. He calls this ''the molecule of the hypochondriac syndrome,'' and he builds his classic monograph about many differing hypochondriacal syndromes around this molecular component. He also devotes considerable attention to what he calls ''the structural elements of the hypochondriac idea,'' namely, the significance of bodily perception, psychic feelings and effects, character traits, constitution and heredity, and organic factors. The mutual relations between these structural elements determine hypochondriacal ideas and the resulting hypochondriacal thinking.

It is instructive to compare and contrast the work of Jahrreiss with Gillespie's. The former starts from an artificially isolated element, namely, a person imagining himself to be ill, and from this he builds his theory of psychopathologically differing hypochondriacal syndromes. Gillespie, on the other hand, attempts to distinguish hypochondria as a clinical and theoretical disease entity from, for example, hysteria and pseudohypochondria, and seems to do so successfully. Unlike Jahrreiss and others, Gillespie believes that hypochondria is always secondary to other disorders and does not exist in a primary, "pure" form. In our view, this represents a basic contradiction in Gillespie's work: to define hypochondria as a disease entity, yet hold it to be always secondary, is not a very cogent idea, even if it is medically acceptable.

On one point it is possible to find consensus. We can describe the manner of involvement in what constitutes the hypochondriacal substance as such a degree of concern and interest that the person in a hypochondriacal mode of being is occupied by this above all other things, paying it continual and—in the absence of strong distracting stimuli—practically exclusive attention. This is often denoted by the term "preoccupation" and in particular "preoccupation with one's bodily or mental condition," which constitutes the matrix of hypochondriacal themes. Correlated with this is a loss of interest in one's total situation in life.

Neither the extreme narcissistic type, nor the type who withdraws into himself because of extreme shyness, nor the autistic person can be called hypochondriacal, although under certain circumstances they may well be likely candidates for hypochondria. The substance of the preoccupied interest and thus a more accurate specification of the *theme of the preoccupation* was implicitly given central importance in many definitions of hypochondria, and by Jahrreiss and Gillespie even explicitly. Hypochondriacs are concerned with a lesion to body or mind, and Jahrreiss divided them into three groups.

1. If a lesion or disorder is thought to be due to a certain disease, he speaks of a "health hypochondriac" (*"Hypochonder um Gesundheit"*) or one who is worried about illness (*"Krankheitskümmerer"*). On the basis of the experience of many practitioners, this condition is focused on the idea of chronic diseases which slowly destroy certain organs and thus insidiously undermine the body. This group also includes the condition of nosophobia, or fear of disease, in which the patient is fearfully preoccupied with anticipated intolerable pain, resulting from an actually existing disease or lesion, for example, from an impending operation, and the fearful concern with the possibility of contracting a disease like epilepsy, cancer, TB, or insanity, which "runs in the family."

2. If the patient fears for his life and is consistently preoccupied with death or dying, Jahrreiss speaks of a "life hypochondriac" (*"ums Leben"*) or one who is worried about death (*"Todeskümmerer"*). One and two are often found in combination, in particular as "heart hypochondria," where a preoccupation with heart and circulation is coupled with fear of dying of a heart attack.

3. This category is reserved for the "beauty hypochondriac," or the person who is worried about being ugly (*"Hässlichkeitskümmerer"*). This person is concerned with his appearance or figure, or some particular aspect of his external appearance. The most common objects of concern, in decreasing order of frequency are: nose, skin, hair, teeth, body weight.

As we have noted earlier, in our view, Jahrreiss's first category properly belongs among the phobias, and does not constitute hypochondria. The second group, again, is a phobia, specifically, "thanatophobia." Only patients in the third group can be regarded as hypochondriacal. Jahrreiss's manner of delimiting and structuring the essence of hypochondria—and this is true of most writers in the field—leads to a terminology that is too broad, too vague. There is a general tendency to use the term "hypochondriacal complaint" glibly whenever a patient seems to make much of bodily symptoms and perceptions. Even though these may go hand in hand with a preoccupation with one's body, they are not enough to justify calling the phenomena hypochondria. For example, the hysteric patient may express his failure to cope with his situation as the fault of his body which "doesn't want to cooperate," or, a patient suffering from neurasthenia may stress the hindrances his body is causing him, yet neither patient is a hypochondriac.

The additional qualification of the true hypochondriac is not based on the nature or intensity of the physical complaints, but on the particular manner in which the patient expresses and interprets these symptoms. Specifically, he believes, despite the absence of clinical evidence, that he is becoming affected by some autonomous agent or force, or by some lesion having become independent; this belief, in turn, determines his whole future attitude toward life, forming an obsession and absorbing all his interests. Not until this stage is reached is the stamp of pure, primary hypochondria impressed on the whole personality.

It is, of course, possible to be clinically ill and hypochondriacal at the same time. In these cases, the hypochondria usually, though not invariably, evolves out of the clinical illness, and should be regarded as secondary. Its symptoms, manifestations, expressions, and self-interpretations are in no way different from those of primary hypochondria, except that they are further affected, often complicated, by the symptoms of the clinical illness, and vice versa.

Aging and old people may also truly experience physical and mental decline as a profound threat, but they are not hypochondriacal as long as, invalid, or ill, they go on living, taking the injury or deformity, the illness and pain, relatively in stride.

Geriatric complaints, disturbed body function, pain, are all warnings, and the body forces the person into occupation, even preoccupation, with that particular aspect of himself. A person who is seriously ill may be afraid, may suspect, or be convinced that he is suffering from or threatened by an incurable illness, and may do all in his power to remove the threat or alleviate the suffering; this, however, is not hypochondria.

The hypochondriacal experience undermines the sufferer's whole life, reduces his potentialities, choices, interests, and plans. He no longer lives for the future, nor does he live in the past; and in the present his vital interests have dwindled to a point of complete identification with his condition.

In clinical illness and invalidism, the patient experiences the feeling of being "broken," of not being able to do as he wishes, of being painfully oppressed and burdened by his body, setting limits to his power of communication and his opportunities. For the seriously ill, or for the person in great pain, the whole experience of life may be concentrated on the particular illness, the particular pain. Yet, the completely introverted nature of the illness may be said to be a *modus vivendi* in its own right, and it is often possible for the patient to develop and realize something of himself in and through his illness, and at times by transcending it.

On the other hand, the hypochondriacal mode of being is determined and formed by the *fascination* of threatening, active, or complete impairment of one's person, alienating the victim from vital activities and possibilities of self-realization. The state of fascination has been described by Ruffin, who said of the hypochondriac that he is imprisoned in a magic circle, where all past and present life is, as it were, sucked into a whirlpool and cut off from the future.

However, the hypochondriacal mode of being has various degrees of intensity, the highest of which has been described above. At a lower degree, we find the fully functioning hypochondriac, who is usually "in the closet," whose condition is kept secret even from most intimate friends and family. His suffering is, nevertheless, exceedingly intense, and his preoccupation is constantly present, just underneath the surface of his otherwise productive, even creative, life. We have previously given many examples of such hypochondriacs, creative artists, more than a few geniuses, who succeeded in converting the energy of the hypochondriacal mode of being to escape from it for periods of time, long enough to allow them artistic expression. The same is true for the noncreative but fully functioning hypochondriac; he goes to work every day, does his job, often extremely well, may well attain executive rank, and no one knows of his preoccupation simmering below the surface. Closet hypochondriacs are, as a rule, useful members of society, and they don't go to doctors; in fact, they invariably mistrust doctors, and when they become clinically ill, they are certain to seek second and third opinions. In the course of the research for this book, it became possible to estimate that the majority of hypochondriacs may belong to this group. It is also possible to speculate that, since doctors and psychiatrists do not see this type of hypochondriac, the entire literature of hypochondria is based on observations of only the most intense hypochondriac who is indeed fully captivated by his "magic circle."

In describing the difficulties surrounding the definitions and classifications of hypochondria, something must be said about the curious category of iatrogenic (physician-caused) hypochondria—a subject of considerable interest during the 1920s, especially in the German literature. Bumke noted that psychiatrists almost daily see patients who owe their hypochondriacal complaints to incautious remarks by a physician. In an apprehensive patient, thoughtless remarks such as "Your arteries are getting clogged," or "Your heart is a bit enlarged," often have devastating results. Such patients may be seriously damaged over a considerable period of years by an otherwise able physician. According to Bumke, even the most excessive masturbation is not as harmful as are remarks sometimes made by physicians to young patients about masturbation, and this holds true for a whole series of medical diagnoses. Most "cardiac neuroses," for example, are but somatic manifestations of anxiety, but when the patient hears the term, he remembers the "cardiac," not the "neurosis." Bumke cites the case of a man who walked without any difficulty with a case of syphilitic aortitis, until a famous internist told him never to go out alone, because he might collapse any minute. This single remark caused severe hypochondria that lasted for seven years.

H. Higier, a contemporary of Bumke's, carried this theme to some excess by listing eleven categories of iatrogenic hypochondria. They are translated and reproduced here mainly for their entertaining quality, yet they do have some tender roots in reality.

1. *Hypochondria pseudosyphilitica* and *hypochondria pseudotuberculosa*, caused by many years of constant fluoroscopic, blood, spinal fluid, and sputum examinations in people once infected, or even never infected, by syphilis or TB.

2. *Hypochondria arteriosclerotica*, caused by repeated suggestions of the presence of presclerotic or arteriosclerotic conditions in patients who tend to complain of chest pain, or have imperfect heart sounds or attacks of vertigo.

3. *Hypochondria hypertonica*, caused by disturbing the psychological equilibrium of patients by measuring and recording every transitory change in blood pressure.

4. *Hypochondria metabolica s. diathetica*, caused by misconceptions produced by the physician about diathesis, constitution, and metabolism.

5. *Hypochondria analytica*, fostered by the physician by repeated analyses of urine and other secretions and excretions, fixing the patient's attention on traces of albumin, spermatozoa, mucus, etc.

6. *Hypochondria diatetica*, caused by the physician who unnecessarily lays down strict dietary rules. This leads the patient to be seriously concerned about even minimal deviations from the prescribed diet to the point of obsession.

7. *Hypochondria balneo-climatica*, occurring in patients with slender means who ignore the "healing powers of nature" (*"vis medicatrix naturae"*) as well as the healing resources available in their own country, and dream—under medical suggestion—of

foreign spas, such as Vichy or Biarritz, imagining them to be the only places where they can be cured.

8. *Hypochondria sexualis*, caused by the physician who attributes every seminal emission, every pain in the prostate, every premature ejaculation, frigidity, or impotence to a gonorrhea long since forgotten.

9. *Hypochondria matrimonialis*, caused by the unnecessary banning by the physician of *coitus reservatus, interruptus*, and *condomatus*, on the grounds that they can cause psychological disorders.

10. *Hypochondria roentgenographica*, the most modern of them all [this was published in 1928], where the despairing patient goes from one radiologist to another, obtaining from each a different and wrong interpretation of an X ray, together with a lecture on such technical terms as cathode rays or Haudek's niches, only to learn at last that the picture shows a perfectly normal condition, and that his only illness is hypochondria, artificially and successfully inoculated into his psyche.

11. *Hypochondria endemica s. sanatorialis*, which, after Thomas Mann, one might call "Magic Mountain Disease"; the artificial atmosphere of the sanatorium, multiple courses of therapy, the attitude of physicians, all create and maintain an aura of disease and provide the patient with an accompanying case of hypochondria. [This is exactly what happens to Hans Castorp, the protagonist in Mann's *The Magic Mountain*.]

After providing his list, Higier concludes: "Although it is true that *Medicus non fit sed nascitur* ("The physician is born, not made"), and that not every conscientious and scientific practitioner knows the art of healing, nevertheless, the old principles of *primum non nocere* ("Above all, do no harm") and *dum spiro spero* ("As long as I breathe, I hope") apply even to the inadequate physician in his contacts with every patient." In actuality, iatrogenic factors have only seldom a direct or decisive effect on hypochondria, which is also true for the habitual reading of medical books and articles. More frequently, iatrogenic factors do contribute to the maintenance and reinforcement of an already established hypochondriacal conviction, mainly in the form of repeated referral of the patient to other practitioners and specialists.

III. HYPOCHONDRIA IN THE PAST:
A Historical and Literary Review

But human bodies are such fools
For all their colleges and schools,
That when no real ills do perplex them,
They make enough themselves to vex them.

—Robert Burns

Little doubt has been left about the fact—and a fact it is—that hypochondria is not one of medicine's success stories. In this chapter, a historical and literary review of what hypochondria meant in former times, it will emerge that, despite a widely varied terminology and a great divergence of points of view, the nature of hypochondria had been more accurately fixed on what Donne called "the strict map of our misery" than it is today. Not that it wasn't always cloaked in ambiguity, aggravated by the additional necessity of translation from different languages; not that it wasn't often beclouded by issues, chiefly religion, that are irrelevant today; not that it wasn't at times the object of ridicule, as it is today; nevertheless, those suffering from it seem to have been better understood, and those attempting to cure it more understanding.

The association of the term "hypochondria" with morbid preoccupation with physical health did not crystallize until the late nineteenth century. Prior to that, it had been variously described as a species of melancholy, "ennui," "spleen," "vapors," and the "English malady." The first work in English devoted entirely to the subject was Timothy Bright's 1586 treatise, which is nothing if not an early essay in psychiatry. The idea that hypochondria was a peculiarly English complaint is an old one:

> Hamlet: Ay, marry, why was he sent to England?
> Clown: Why, because he was mad. He shall recover his wits there; or if he do not, it is of no great matter there.
> Hamlet: Why?'
> Clown: 'Twill not be seen in him;
> There the men are as mad as he.

This idea is attested to by the publication of a work called *The English Malady* by Dr. George Cheyne in 1733, which is richly documented by the author's physical suffering. Burton's *Anatomy of Melancholy,* published nearly a hundred years before Cheyne's work, also made clear the close association between melancholy and hypochondria. Burton includes a category of hypochondriacal or flatuous melancholy, the symptoms of which include:

> . . . besides fear and sorrow, sharp belchings, fulsome crudities, heat in the bowels, wind and rumblings in the gut, vehement gripings, pain in the belly and stomach . . . cold sweat . . . cold joints . . . indigestion . . . They cannot endure their own fulsome belchings . . . midriff and bowels are pulled up, the veins about their eyes look red, and swell from vapours and wind . . .

These samplings, drawn from English sources only, support the acuity of Gillespie's definition of hypochondria, which emphasizes that it is a preoccupation with *physical or mental* disorder, but as our review of classical attitudes will show, the ancients were more interested in the mental, spiritual aspects, or ennui.

The origins of the word "ennui" have been much disputed, and various derivations have been proposed. The accepted etymology seems to be that ennui stems from the Latin *odium* or *odio,* and most probably from the expression, *esse in odio* ("to be an object of hate"). It has been tentatively defined by Reinhard Kuhn as the "state of emptiness that the soul feels when it is deprived of interest in action, life, and the world," a condition that is the immediate consequence of an encounter with nothingness, and has as an immediate effect a disaffection with reality.

Literature, both ancient and modern, shows this definition to be deficient in its neglect of physical characteristics. First, it is clear that ennui affects both the "soul" and body and that its manifestations are both spiritual and physical. To emphasize the physical aspects of ennui, Baudelaire often used the English word "spleen." Flaubert, in his letters to Louise Colet, speaks of the "nausea of ennui" and frequently refers to it as a "leprosy of the soul." In *Being and Nothingness,* Sartre makes it clear that ennui is not merely a metaphor for a sort of spiritual revulsion but the same physical disgust that leads to vomiting.

The second circumstance that associates ennui with hypochondria is that both are independent of our will, and, finally, the condition is usually characterized by estrangement, or alienation, which psychiatrists today almost invariably associate with hypochondria.

One would expect to find ennui to be clearly present in the ethical writings of the Greek philosophers, but here we come to our first terminological differences. Although ennui as such is absent from the work of Aristotle, the related concept of melancholy is found within a definite framework that was to be adopted by many future writers and was to have an impact on medieval and Renaissance thought and literature. This framework consists of the division of the formative influences on man into the four "humors." The variant mixtures of what were then considered bodily fluids, the differing proportions among blood, phlegm, choler (or yellow bile), and melancholy (or black bile), were considered as determining the character of man, as the shaping forces of his physical and mental qualities and his emotional disposition.

It is to the black bile, whose preponderance determines the

melancholic nature, that Aristotle devotes an important section of his *Problemata Physica*. The initial proposition of this treatise, and the assumption on which it is based, is that all extraordinary men in philosophy, politics, poetry, and the arts are melancholics—a concept of the genius that was to have an immeasurable influence on literature right up to the present.

But the black bile can also be virulent. In its most concentrated form, it can lead to the infliction of the most extreme form of violence on oneself and on others. Aristotle cites the example of the melancholic Heracles, who in an excess of fury slaughters his children by Megara, and who later tears open his wounds before his self-immolation. Senseless physical suffering and the most excruciating pain as a reaction against ennui became a prevalent theme in the Elizabethan theater, in the Romantic period, as well as in twentieth-century literature and psychiatry. Samuel Beckett's hoboes, clawing at their oozing sores, are relatives of the Spartan Lysander, whom Aristotle also mentions as an example of a melancholic who destroys himself, and also of the numerous masochists in the psychiatric literature.

Perhaps the most important aspect of the black bile to be discussed in the *Problemata* is that which has to do with the creative process—another strikingly modern psychiatric theme. Melancholy can have diametrically opposite consequences. On the one hand, it can lead to the artistic sterility from which Mallarmé and many others were to suffer; on the other hand, it can be the force that inspired many writers, such as Proust.

The most serious treatment accorded to the problem of ennui in antiquity is to be found in Seneca's dialogue, *Concerning the Tranquility of the Soul*. Indeed, the beginning of this treatise resembles nothing so much as a psychiatric consultation. In the first chapter, Serenus, the interlocutor, attempts a clear description of his state of mind: "I find that most often I am neither free of the things I hate and fear, nor, on the other hand, am I in bondage to them." In the hope that Seneca will find a name and a cure for the malady, Serenus enumerates his three major symptoms, all of which are contradictory. First, he speaks of his predilection for frugality and simplicity. He is not a gourmet and is happier with simple foods and plain service. However, without explanation, from time to time he suddenly finds himself fascinated by all forms of luxury. He devours rich banquets served by well-appointed slaves, and is taken by all forms of ostentation.

His second problem is of the same nature. He has enthusiasm for public affairs, but, again, he finds himself at times drawn in the other direction; he hurries back home and decides to lead the life of leisure. Then, as he picks up a book to read, its content exults him, and, fired with enthusiasm, he can hardly wait to hasten back to the Forum.

Serenus's third contradiction is found in his intellectual life. Whenever he sits down to write, he decides to do it for himself alone, without thought of future publication. But no sooner does he put pen to paper, he begins to polish his sentences as if writing to attain immortality, and he can think only of his future readers. "I am distressed," concludes Serenus, "not by the storm but by the seasickness."

In his reply, Seneca speaks of "the torpor of the spirit," in which inaction and one's impatience with it lead to the drowning of passions and feelings—a very modern notion, expressed best in Sartre's *No Exit*. He counsels that solitude and social life should be carefully balanced, and that the same equilibrium should be maintained between work and leisure.

Seneca's advice bears a striking parallel to advice Dr. Samuel Johnson was to give some seventeen centuries later on the same subject. Boswell tells us:

> He mentioned to me now, for the first time, that he had been distrest by melancholy, and for that reason had been obliged to fly from study and meditation, to the dissipating variety of life. Against melancholy he recommended constant occupation of mind, a great deal of exercise, moderation in eating and drinking, and especially to shun drinking at night. He said melancholy people were apt to fly to intemperance for relief, but that it sunk them much deeper in misery. He observed, that labouring men who work hard, and live sparingly, are seldom or never troubled with low spirits.

Melancholy, indeed, should be diverted, [he says elsewhere] by
every means but drinking.

It is difficult to see how a contemporary psychotherapist, even
one specializing in behavior modification, would advise a patient
with the complaints of Serenus in a significantly different fashion.

Nor did Seneca ignore the possibility of suicide in the melancholic person. "There are many," he says, "who do not consider
life painful, merely superfluous." The most likely candidates for
suicide among melancholics are those who are, or imagine they
are, doing and seeing the same things, which results in a sense of
futility, and eventually in a disgust for life. Seneca rules out
suicide as a possible exit, calling it "ridiculous," even though it
was far from uncommon in his day.

It should not be concealed from the reader that Seneca was
not in the mainstream of the thought of his times in regard to
matters of psychology. The majority of his contemporaries and
those who followed him were largely unaware of the existence of
ennui. Cicero, for example, even rejected the Aristotelian proposition of the talented nature of melancholics, and would have had
little patience for or understanding of Serenus's state of mind.

A rapid survey of classical literature and philosophy indicates that while the concept of ennui was not unknown to the
ancients, the paucity of examples suggests that the idea did not
occupy the important position it has assumed in more modern
times. Perhaps there is some truth to the image we have of the
classical spirit as one of tranquility, harmony, and lucidity. And
yet the darker side of the Greek spirit cannot be denied. In *Some
Aspects of the Greek Genius,* Samuel H. Butcher convincingly
demonstrates the pervasive influence of melancholy in Greek
culture. There can be certainly no question that the Achilles
depicted in the *Iliad* is afflicted with a profound sorrow, and many
Greek poems bear the mark of a certain ennui. Nevertheless, the
melancholy of Greeks and Romans never went too far; it was
outweighed by a joy of existence that is the very opposite of
ennui. In other words, if the ancients were aware of ennui, they

did not consider it a fit subject for literature and carefully hid it in the shadows. Both the Stoic and Epicurean ideals preferred not to delve into the darker sentiments of men, even if Nietzsche was to claim in *The Birth of Tragedy* that "the whole being of Greek man, despite his beauty and harmony, bridged an unseen abyss of sorrow."

In the early Christian era, ennui became a key idea that continued to develop in importance and complexity through the Dark and Middle Ages. In the radically different psychological framework of Christianity, ennui, formerly a notion of minor importance, was elevated to the status of one of the capital sins, of which hypochondria's position today is a surviving remnant.

There was, to begin with, a proliferation of names for the single concept of ennui/melancholy. *Siccitas,* or dryness of the soul, denoted a state of aridity that leads to complete spiritual impotence. *Tristitia,* or inexplicable sorrow, was akin to the nostalgic longing for a lost kingdom of the Romantics. *Desidia* meant a complete paralysis of the will that had as a consequence the inability to work—a very modern condition. On a simpler level, there was *pigritia,* which simply meant laziness. In the end, however, one word came to dominate and eventually succeed all the others: *acedia* (or accidie), signifying lack of interest, became the recognized and accepted definition for a condition of the soul characterized by torpor, dryness, and indifference, culminating in a disgust concerning anything to do with the spiritual life.

While the Greeks and Romans, too, had been fond of making lists of various vices, an equivalent to acedia is not to be found on any of them. In contrast, when one of the best-known early Christian mystics, Evagrius of Pontus, composed one of the earliest, perhaps even the first, of Christian lists of capital sins, *Of the Eight Capital Sins,* acedia is given the longest and most detailed treatment. Although most of the early mystics accorded acedia an important place, only a few set it apart in as radical a fashion as did Evagrius. Eventually, Gregory the Great established the list of capital sins as it was to prevail to this day, not only in number but in order; by merging tristitia and acedia, he reduced the list to seven sins. As Kierkegaard was to note in his *Journal* (July 20, 1839), "What we call 'spleen,' the mystics knew under the name tristitia and the Middle Ages under the name acedia. . . . It shows a deep knowledge of the human nature that Gregory should have included it among the seven capital sins." As a marginal comment, Kierkegaard adds, "That is what my father called 'a silent despair.' " In this single comment, acedia, ennui, and melancholy are united. (To equate acedia, ennui, and melancholy—all forerunners of hypochondria—is by no means farfetched. Balzac used acedia and ennui interchangeably, as did Baudelaire in one of his autobiographical segments. Flaubert, in a letter to Turgenev, described the ennui that led to his artistic production as being identical to what the mystics called "the state of aridity.")

During the half a millennium that separated Gregory from the High Middle Ages, there was little, if any, development in the concept of acedia. While there were numerous literary analyses of the seven deadly sins, commentaries on acedia hardly go beyond the depiction developed by Evagrius. Despite its virulence, acedia remained a fairly unchanging phenomenon during the course of the many centuries that separate the first desert fathers from Saint Thomas Aquinas. Although, thanks to Gregory, the lay public was not entirely unfamiliar with it, it was not until Petrarch and the advent of the Renaissance that acedia became secularized and turned into a universal affliction. Even in the Middle Ages, there were secular exceptions. A sorrowful strain is manifest in the romances of Chrétien de Troyes, and Wolfram von Eschenbach depicts his Parzival as a melancholic. Charles d'Orléans, who described himself as "the most dolorous in France," was capable of a precise analysis of his malady, ranging from simple indolence to total despair in his lyric poetry. "Enough, enough," he cried out, "more than enough. Have you not had enough?" Within the melancholy espoused in the works of Charles d'Orléans and his contemporaries are contained the germs of the "Elizabethan malady" that was to ravage all of Europe.

Petrarch was undoubtedly the first modern writer, and his works—and life—were dominated by a virulent form of ennui; in them, medieval acedia becomes secularized and makes the transition to its modern form. In his prose writings in Latin, we find one of the deepest and most subjective depictions of the state of ennui, whereas in his Italian lyrics this anguish is given poetic and sometimes allegorical form and becomes in a way depersonalized.

Petrarch's autobiographical *Secretum*, which is primarily devoted to the topic, is one of the first pieces of modern confessional writing and is closer in spirit to the *Confessions* of Rousseau than to those of Saint Augustine, even though the latter had a great influence on its conception. It is cast in the form of an imaginary dialogue between Franciscus and Augustinius, presided over by Lady Truth, and it quickly becomes evident that Augustinius is Petrarch's alter ego. The interlocutors are two facets of the same personality, the accuser and the accused, and it is through their interaction that the actual subject of the confessions emerges. The dialogue between them is one between the self and the self, as it is in Beckett's *Waiting for Godot*. Franciscus has been stricken by a long and dangerous malady, and when he is told by Augustinius that he is the victim of a terrible scourge of the soul, melancholy, also known as acedia, Franciscus is overcome by a violent fit of trembling, proceeds to condemn himself, and refuses all consolation. What is worse, *he takes a terrible delight in his own suffering,* and we see voluptuousness of suffering *(voluptas dolendi)* in its purest form. It is in the *Secretum* that Petrarch expresses in the most eloquent terms everything essential he has to say about a condition which is an amalgam between medieval acedia and modern melancholy. In his other Latin writings we find but isolated depictions of traits that were already commonplace in antiquity.

Whereas the *Secretum* is an expression of *mental* melancholy, Petrarch's Italian poems, inspired by his encounter with the immortalized Laura in 1327, are sweet complaints by comparison, yet remarkably laced with expressions of *physical* complaints. Words like "tired," "weak," "heavy," "fatigued," "frail," recur constantly. "Weak is the thread to which my heavy

life is attached," is a typical opening line of these poems which
Petrarch himself described as "dolorous rhymes" written in a
"tired and frail style."

The themes detected in the writings of Petrarch were subsequently exploited with brilliance by the French poets of the
sixteenth century who cast off the last vestiges of their medieval
heritage. Two centuries after Petrarch, Marot wrote lines such as,
"I languish, I am heavy with sorrow," and, as in the case of
Petrarch, love is no cure for melancholy. "Mourning and ennui
are the only gifts" that affection for a mistress can bring the poet.
Marot, too, saw in his suffering a voluptuous delight: "What
pleases me is a dolorous sentiment."

There is an inevitability about the poet's malady; he tells us
he was born in the state of ennui. It is no longer an acquired
characteristic, a vice, or a bad habit that he can divest himself of
with an effort of the will or the help of God. We have previously
seen ennui in the guise of a mortal sin, a temptation, and even an
inspiration; now it makes its first appearance as a fatality.

Ennui is the common theme in the verses of most of Marot's
contemporaries, Scève and the poetess Louise Labé, who
shocked the censorious spirits of the sixteenth century—among
them Calvin himself who berated her as "meretricious"—by a
mode of life that exemplified an early form of sexual liberation.

Medieval and early Renaissance melancholy, characterized
by morbid mental and physical depression, was an Italian and
French product that reached the shores of England relatively late,
exported there by the increasing number of travelers around
the middle of the sixteenth century. That it was first regarded as a
"foreign trait" is indicated by the fact that its two earliest
personifications, Shakespeare's Jaques and Hamlet were French
and Danish. Once this contagious disease had crossed the Chan-
nel, it established itself rapidly, and, Lawrence Babb, a keen
scholar of Elizabethan society, tells us, it was a common and
widespread malady by 1580. The court of Elizabeth, dominated
by an atmosphere of intrigue, proved to be a fertile breeding
ground for all sorts of neuroses, and the "melancholy malcon-

tent," as he was most often called, became a stock figure in life and literature.

References to melancholy in both medical and literary works are countless during the Elizabethan period, and the variety of forms it assumed ranged from simple indolence to despair, from lovesickness to metaphysical anguish, from longing to spiritual and physical paralysis. Not surprisingly, it was Shakespeare who exploited the spectrum of melancholy and demonstrated its complexities.

One of his accomplishments was to fix once and for all the traits of the "splenetic" gentleman as he existed in late sixteenth-century England, and he did this in his apparent caricature of the melancholy Jaques, one of the attendant lords of the exiled duke in *As You Like It*. As he has no essential function within the comedy, it is likely that Shakespeare included him because the theatergoing public would recognize him as a stock figure who reassured and pleased them.

Jaques's most obvious trait is his hypersensitivity. He is first shown sitting at the edge of a stream, "augmenting it with tears." He is grieving over the wounding of a hunted deer. Another trait on which Shakespeare insists is Jaques's compulsive need to verbalize his melancholy. His copious tears are matched by "a thousand similes" through which he expresses his sentiments, although he consistently shuns his fellows and communicates in verbose monologues. A third characteristic of Jaques's ennui is that it represents for him a source of pleasure. Jaques revels in music, not because it abates his melancholy, but rather because it intensifies it: "I can suck melancholy out of a song as a weasel sucks eggs."

There seem to be no external causes to explain Jaques's melancholy; it results from a vision of existence in which everything is rendered meaningless. He elucidates this in his demonstration of the insignificance of life: "All the world's a stage, / And all the men and women merely players," he proclaims, and then goes on to describe the seven acts of which the farce of life is composed, beginning with "the infant, / Mewling and puking in

the nurse's arms," and ending with "second childishness and
mere oblivion, / Sans teeth, sans eyes, sans taste, sans everything." Here, as elsewhere, Jaques reveals that he is not merely a
caricature of a melancholic, but that his exaggerated affectations
may be but a mask that hides the real melancholic. He is the
disillusioned traveler who has seen and learned too much.

In Hamlet, Jaques's symptoms take on tragic dimensions.
Like Jaques's mannerisms, Hamlet's ostentatious display of woe
is a spectacle, a show put on to hide a deeper inner desolation:
"How weary, stale, flat and unprofitable / Seem to me all the uses
of this world." This bitter awareness is the basis of the self-
analysis he presents to Rosencrantz and Guildenstern:

> . . . I have of late, but wherefore I know not, lost all my mirth,
> forgone all custom of exercises; and indeed it goes so heavily with
> my disposition that this goodly frame, the earth, seems to me a
> sterile promontory; this most excellent canopy, the air, look you,
> this brave o'erhanging firmament, this majestical roof fretted with
> golden fire, why, it appears no other thing to me than a foul and
> pestilent congregation of vapours. What a piece of work is man!
> how noble in reason! how infinite in faculty! in form and moving
> how express and admirable! in action how like an angel! in ap-
> prehension how like a god! the beauty of the world! the paragon of
> animals! And yet, to me, what is this quintessence of dust? man
> delights not me.

In *Richard II*, Shakespeare deals with the very substance of
ennui. Just after the king has left for battle, the queen confides in
the servant Bushy who chided her for being "too much sad." She
explains that it is beyond her will to resist it: "Some unborn
sorrow, ripe in fortune's womb, / Is coming towards me, and my
inward soul / With nothing trembles; at some thing it grieves /
More than with parting from my lord the king."

Shakespeare presents the queen as a victim of ennui from the
beginning. In contrast, Richard II is a natural activist who is
gradually overtaken by ennui and eventually succumbs to it.
When he learns of the treachery of presumably loyal friends, his

initial rage is succeeded by a discouragement that threatens to overwhelm him for the first time. He rejects all action, and in his depression wants to do nothing to defend himself. Consequently, he allows himself to be deposed by a man who had not the slightest intention of deposing him. He lets the crowd throw dust at him, and finally lets himself be imprisoned. This sapping of the vital forces by ennui is best summed up in a phrase from *Romeo and Juliet:* "Dry sorrow drinks our blood." Ennui, like a vampire, drained the blood of Richard II until he could no longer find pleasure even in the despair of nothingness, until only death could comfort him.

Later writers subjected melancholy to meticulous dissection, with more and more attention being paid to the medical aspects, and reaching the conclusion that melancholy was like a cancerous growth not easy to arrest; only all-consuming distractions could save its victims from total despair.

On his last voyage Swift's Gulliver encounters the Houyhnhnms, a noble race that incorporates all human virtues and is exempt from all human vices. Their lives are guided entirely by the ideal of the eighteenth century, pure reason. There lives on the same island a race of repugnant simians, the bestial Yahoos, whom Gulliver considers as the most odious of all the beings he has come across during his travels. One of the peculiar characteristics of these foul and brutal creatures is that they are subject to a sort of crisis incomprehensible to the Houyhnhnms. The symptoms of this malady are groans and cries, and its victims become irritable and seek to withdraw from the company of others. The Houyhnhnms, despite their lucidity, could find no cause for this affliction, but they had found one remedy that never failed, namely, to put the victims to hard labor. Swift leaves no doubt in the reader's mind: the Yahoos, of whom he bitterly admits to being one, are the human race. Their malady is the spleen.

Spleen, which has always had wider linguistic currency in England than ennui, was by common consent regarded as a

peculiarly British trait. Dr. George Cheyne, himself plagued by
the affliction, acknowledges the validity of this attribution—
which he blames on the miserable weather—in the prefatory
explanation of the title of his medical discourse, *The English
Malady:* "The Title I have chosen for this Treatise, is a Reproach
universally thrown on this Island by Foreigners, by whom
Spleen, Vapours, and Lowness of Spirits, are in Derision, called
the English Malady. And I wish there were not so good Grounds
for this Reflection." In the *Spectator,* Addison states that "Melancholy is a kind of Demon that haunts our Island"; medical
treatises devoted to spleen proliferated, and it was frequently
dealt with in the pages of the *Tatler,* the *Guardian,* and the
Spectator, where it was frequently satirized by both Addison and
Steele.

The concept of human nature which the Renaissance inherited from Aristotle has at least one thing in common with that
of modern science: the assumption that body and mind are closely
related and mutually influential. Renaissance psychology is a
physiological psychology, tending to explain mental conditions in
terms of physical causes and vice versa; in point of fact, physiology and psychology were more inseparable than they are today
and represented at least a temporary suspension of the Judeo-
Christian split between the two.

The principles of this physiological psychology were widely
disseminated in sixteenth- and early seventeenth-century
England. Many treatises on the subject, some of them transla-
tions, others original works by Englishmen, appeared in the
native language. Poets did their share toward instructing their
countrymen; Spenser's *Faerie Queene* contains an anatomy of
human nature, several expository poems are entirely devoted to
the nature of man, and various plays present the accepted psychology in allegorical form. One gets the impression that England
of the time of Elizabeth and the early Stuarts thought a great deal
about its physical and psychic states.

In order to understand the evolution of the variously named
physical and psychic states—ennui, spleen, melancholy,

hypochondria, and so forth—and how these states came to be categorized into present concepts of illness, including hypochondria, it will be necessary to review briefly the principles of Renaissance psychology and physiology, simplifying and occasionally ignoring in the process numerous disagreements about details.

We have already touched upon the Aristotelian view of physiology, which formed the basis of the Elizabethan one. The soul was the force which animated the inert matter of the body and directed its activities. It was one and indivisible. It was, nevertheless, for purposes of analysis and description, divided into three subsouls known as the "vegetative," the "sensitive" (or "sensible"), and the "rational" souls.

The vegetative soul was seated in the liver; its principal faculties were nourishment, growth, and reproduction. In general, it directed the humbler physiological processes below the level of consciousness. Plants, animals, as well as men have vegetative souls.

The sensitive soul had the faculties of feeling and motion. It had the power of perceiving objects other than itself, it evaluated them as pleasing or repellent, and it directed motions of the body either to approach or to avoid them. It was seated in the brain and heart, and animals as well as men were endowed with it.

Man was distinguished from all other created things by the possession of the rational soul, located in the brain, which was capable of distinguishing good from evil, of contemplating itself, and of knowing God. In modern terms, the rational soul is equivalent to the "self."

The physical life of man rested on two pillars, that is, heat and moisture with which the body was endowed at birth—another Aristotelian notion. As man grew older, his body became gradually drier and colder. When the natural moisture was consumed and the natural heat failed, one died. Thus, heat and moisture were conducive to life, and cold and dryness were hostile.

The Renaissance term for digestion was "concoction." The liver, a hot organ, was to the stomach as fire under a pot. The product of digestion in the stomach was a viscid, whitish fluid called "chyle." This was conveyed to the liver where it underwent a second "concoction," the products of which were the four primary humors. The most plentiful of these was blood. Mingled with the blood produced by the liver was a light and effervescent fluid, "choler," which tended to rise. There was also a heavy and sluggish fluid called "melancholy," which tended to sink. Melancholy consisted of the less pure and less nutritious parts of the chyle and was considered semiexcremental. The fourth humor, "phlegm," was merely chyle half-digested. Phlegm further digested by the liver would be blood. Each humor had two qualities: blood was hot and moist, choler was hot and dry, melancholy was cold and dry, and phlegm was cold and moist. The four humors are therefore analogous to the four elements: air is hot and moist, fire hot and dry, earth cold and dry, and water cold and moist. The humors also had secondary qualities: blood was red and sweet; choler was yellow, bitter, thin, and volatile; melancholy was black, sour, thick, and heavy; and phlegm was whitish or colorless, tasteless, and watery.

Illnesses were due to humoral abnormalities: to superabundance or deficiency of a humor throughout the body, to improper concentration of a humor in one organ, or to the presence somewhere in the body of noxious, unnatural forms of choler, phlegm, or melancholy. Renaissance medicine explains every illness by one of these conditions. Each illness was classified as hot and dry, cold and dry, and so forth, according to the offending humor.

The fundamental principle of cure was the restoration of the normal. The most drastic method was bloodletting to evacuate the injurious humor from the veins. Purgation was supposed to serve the same purpose. Certain drugs were specific purgatives for certain humors. Black hellebore, for example, was the favorite purgative for melancholy; rhubarb for choler. Various medicines are used to change the character of a humor by moistening, drying, heating, cooling, thickening, thinning. Diet was important. A patient suffering from a hot and dry disease should eat cold and moist foods, such as lettuce and watercress. In Renaissance dietaries, the various foods are described in terms of heat, cold, moisture, and dryness, so that the reader may choose those foods that have a nature opposite to that of his complaint.

The patient's daily life must also be regulated. Idleness and sleep warm and moisten the body; labor and walking cool and dry it. Temperature and humidity of weather must be taken into account. The patient should enjoy peace of mind, for mental perturbation breeds ill humors.

The ideal man would have the four humors mingled in his body in exact proportion. Blood would be the most abundant humor, phlegm the next, melancholy the next, the choler the least. Such a man would enjoy perfect health of body and mind and would be richly endowed with capabilities and virtues. In actuality, each man's constitution varied more or less from the norm by a surplus of one humor or another; and his complexion, or temperament, was designated according to the dominant humor as sanguine, choleric, phlegmatic, or melancholic. The sanguine complexion was regarded as the most desirable, primarily because heat and moisture are the qualities of life. The melancholic temperament was usually considered the least enviable, for cold and dryness are opposite to the vital qualities. A man of hot and moist temperament was young at sixty; one of cold and dry temperament was old at forty.

The dominant humor to a large extent determines the individual's appearance and behavior. The well-informed observer can readily classify men according to their complexions. A sanguine man is fleshy, ruddy, fair-haired, amiable of countenance and manner, kindly, liberal, fond of good food, wine, and music, amorous, intelligent, courageous. The choleric person is lean, hairy, rash, quick to anger, proud, revengeful, bold, ambitious, shrewd. The phlegmatic man is short and fat, pale, torpid, slothful, mentally dull. Melancholic men are, as Lemnius puts it in his *The Touchstone of Complexions,* "lean, dry, lank . . . the face becommeth pale, yellowish and swarthy. . . . As touching the

notes and markes of their minds, they are churlish, whyning . . .
obstinate, greedy . . . they use a certaine slow pace and soft nyce
gayte, holding downe their heads, with countenance and loke . . .
grim and frowninge." They are taciturn, they love to be alone,
and they are continually tormented by fears and sorrows. Of all
the four complexions, the sanguine is the happiest, the melancholic the most miserable. The sanguine man is the most attractive in appearance, whereas the "most deformed is the Melancholick."

Renaissance scholars were notoriously fond of analogies.
One finds a very complex system of analogies built around the
four humors and the four complexions. The correspondence
between the elements and the humors is only one of several. For
example, the planet Saturn, the earth, the north wind, winter, old
age, and the melancholic temperament, are all cold and dry. In
turn, Saturn, the north wind, winter, and old age cause increase in
the melancholic humor in all men.

Among these various associations, that which connects
melancholy with Saturn probably appears more often than any
other in Renaissance scientific and literary works. One finds it in
astrological treatises. According to one astrologer, Saturn is
"cold and drie, melancholick, earthie, masculine . . . malevolent,
destroyer of life." The astrological characterization of the saturnine man (one born under Saturn's influence) corresponds closely
with the usual conception of the melancholic man. "Saturnine"
and "melancholic" are virtually synonymous.

The melancholic character of old age and the consequent
decrepitude of the aged receive considerable attention in learned
works. An affliction "natural to all, and which no man living can
avoid," says Robert Burton, "is old age, which being cold and
dry, and of the same quality as Melancholy is, must needs cause
it, by diminution of spirits and substance." Since melancholy is
the humor most inimical to life, old men are subject to the most
grievous infirmities of body and mind. Scholarly writers show
deep concern for the hard lot of the aged, and in works like André
Du Laurens' essay, "Of Old Age," Thomas Newton's *The Old*

Mans Dietarie, and Simon Goulart's *The Wise Vieillard,* they offer advice on how to mitigate the evils of senility.

So close was the interaction between mind and body in the Renaissance view of Elizabethan England that there was no need for coining terms like psychosomatic or hypochondriacal in their present usage. Everything that happened in the mind, also happened in the body, and vice versa. For example, a passion was a definite sensation, felt first in the heart and subsequently throughout the body. Desire and joy are agreeable sensations. A joyful heart, says Melanchthon, dilates with pleasure as if to embrace the object of its joy. In sorrow, the heart suffered painful contraction. When the heart is "stricken and beaten with some unpleasant thing . . . then doth it retire, close up itself and feele griefe, as if it had received a wound." Sorrow was physical pain. In anger, the heart swelled belligerently and sent forth blood to repel the offending object. It grew hot and inflamed the blood, and the whole body trembled, even the bones.

Passions had a considerable influence upon physical health. Joy was "a medicine to the body. Physicians always exhort sicke persons to be as merry as they may, and to avoid sorrow and sadnesse, which being colde and dry is contrary to life, and so consumeth men."

Any immoderate passion might be harmful. Anger stirred up natural heat and inflamed the blood. Even joy was harmful if excessive, and any passion, if it was very sudden and violent, might kill outright. As a result of furious anger, "some have broken their veines, supprest their urine, whereby death hath ensued." In violently expanding or contracting the heart, a passion might break the heart strings.

The Renaissance physiology of passions has contributed many common phrases to the English language. Phrases such as "ardent love," "blazing anger," "boiling blood," "chilling fear," "cold-blooded murder," and "broken heart," were not figures of speech as they are now. Also, when we describe someone today as "sanguine," "choleric," "phlegmatic," or "melancholic," we mean something very close to what the

Elizabethans meant by the same adjectives, although they have lost their medical connotations.

There is much to be learned by today's physicians, by hypochondriacs, and by the seriously ill, from the Renaissance belief that man's greatest enemies lie within himself and that his greatest task is self-mastery. Before self-mastery must come self-knowledge, for no man can govern his "lower nature" without an understanding of it. For this reason, treatises on psychology echoed with the ancient exhortation: *Nosce teipsum*— know thyself! Melanchthon's *Liber de Anima,* Rogers's *Anatomie of the Minde,* Wright's *Passions of the Minde,* Charron's *Of Wisdome,* Sir John Davies' *Nosce Teipsum,* Mornay's *True Knowledge a Mans Owne Selfe,* Walkington's *Optick Glasse of Humors,* Reynolds's *Treatise of the Passions,* and many other works, have the avowed purpose of instructing the reader on the subject of his own nature, so that he may be armed with the knowledge which is necessary to virtue and happiness. More interestingly, the quality of most of these treatises, both in style and content, far surpasses that of today's self-help, inspirational books.

He who "thoroughly would know himself, must as well knowe his bodie, as his minde," advises Rogers. Instruction in psychology necessarily includes instruction in physiology and in the means of maintaining physical health. Treatment of diseases of the soul may involve, first of all, cure of diseases of the body. A temperate mind is not likely to be found in a distempered body: "the temperance or intemperance that may be in our bodies, exdendeth itself into the estate of our soule." Clearly, the Renaissance physician shared the responsibility of the moral teacher, and many were quite conscious of it and dealt with it with seriousness.

It was during this period that melancholy, which, one must keep in mind, was always a synonym for hypochondria, was first seen as a physical, as well as a psychological condition. It was beginning to be used to designate a disease due to the presence of a melancholy humor abnormal in quantity or quality. The species most frequently listed are "head melancholy," "body melancholy," and "hypochondriacal melancholy." The distinction between the first two does not seem very useful, for the causes, symptoms, and cure of the one are never clearly differentiated from those of the other. The psychological symptoms of all three are very similar.

The causes of this malady included everything that might engender a melancholy humor. Diet was a frequent cause. Burton, for example, condemns beef as a food that breeds "gross melancholy blood," along with virtually all other varieties of meat. He quotes Pliny approvingly: "Simple diet is best; heaping up of several meats is pernicious, and sauces worse; many courses bring many diseases." After quoting virtually hundreds of ancient authors for the same effect, Burton declares: *"Plures crapula quam gladius"* ("Gluttony kills more than the sword").

Other causes were the climate, one's abode, too much or too little sleep. Either idleness or overexertion might engender natural melancholy; the former caused the blood to become thick, while the latter dried it excessively. Intense thinking was known to be a psychological cause of melancholy. While the mind was active, nature neglected the stomach and liver, with the result that digestion was poor and its product melancholic. Also, the physical inactivity that accompanied mental labor hindered proper evacuation, and the mind consequently became sorrowful and fearful.

Scholars necessarily were inclined to melancholy because of their arduous mental activity and their sedentary life; melancholy was the scholar's occupational disease. Men of letters, says Marsilio Ficino in his *De Vita*, either are melancholy by innate temperament or become so through study. One may add, as Renaissance writers did not, that poverty, disillusionment, and discouragement all contributed to the scholar's melancholy. The days were long past when intellectual achievement was encouraged and rewarded by great patrons like Augustus Caesar and Maecenas. In the Renaissance, scholarly life was mostly one of sorrow and hardship, and both of these breed melancholy.

Burton includes in his *Anatomy* a long discourse on "love of
learning, or overmuch study" as a cause of melancholy, "with a
digression of the misery of scholars, and why the Muses are
Melancholy." In dealing with these subjects, he displays considerable personal feeling: "How many poor scholars have lost
their wits, or become dizzards, neglecting all worldly affairs and
their own health . . . to gain knowledge!"

The melancholic malady might be due to any circumstance
that produced black bile. It might also be due to functional failure
in any one of a group of abdominal organs known collectively as
the *hypochondria,* or *hypochondries.* These include notably the
liver, gallbladder, spleen, and uterus. When melancholy was a
consequence of disorder in any hypochondriacal organ, it was
called "hypochondriacal melancholy."

The spleen was the most frequent seat of this condition. The
spleen is a spongy structure in the lower left side, and it was
supposed to absorb all superfluous black bile from the liver and
blood. It used the more nutritive part of the bile to nourish itself,
discharged a part into the stomach to provoke appetite, and
excreted the rest. Sometimes, however, "either for feeblenesse
or obstruction," the spleen failed "to suck the melancholie from
the blood." Sometimes, moreover, through loss of its capacity to
excrete, the spleen swelled and exuded melancholy into the
veins. The swollen spleen had become a cesspool, a festering
humor, from which the black vapors ascended. Medical writers
manifested no small disgust with the spleen: "This member of the
whole bodie is the grossest and evil favouredst to be held, blacke
of colour, and evil savorie of taste."

Humors that were confined and compressed within a narrow
space were believed to putrefy and generate heat. When melancholy was imprisoned within the spleen, it was likely to become
hot, and this heated melancholy was pervaded by gas. The idea
that hot melancholic humors were "windy" seems to be based on
an analogy with boiling water. The heated humor, "coming as it
were to boyle, is puffed up and sendeth his vapours into all the
parts neere thereabout." If the spleen failed to discharge itself,

therefore, there was an unnatural boiling of heat, with windiness on the left side. The frontispiece of Burton's *Anatomy*, which represents various types of melancholy men, depicts a picture of "Hypochondriacus," who is bent toward the left. Because the hot melancholic humors involved were gaseous, hypochondriacal melancholy is often called "windy" or "flatulent" melancholy.

Organs other than the spleen might be the seat of hypochondriacal melancholy. Du Laurens informs us that, next to the spleen, the liver and the mesentery are most frequently at fault. Some authors mention a uterine melancholy, and there are other varieties. In any case, most hypochondriacs "feele a burning in the places called Hypochondria, they heare continually a noyse and rumbling sound throughout all their bellie, they are beaten with winde on both sides," concludes Du Laurens.

Hypochondriacal melancholy is notable among melancholies for the fact that it furnished the late seventeenth century with a set of terms. By the time of Queen Anne, "melancholy" as the name for morbid depression had been largely replaced by "hypochondria," "spleen," "hysteria," and "vapours," all four terms denoting the same disorder.

A recapitulation at this point might be helpful. "Melancholy," as it was used in Renaissance scientific literature, was a word of many meanings and implications. It meant, first of all, a cold, dry humor which was normally present in the body. This was "natural melancholy." The word might also designate blood, choler, phlegm, or natural melancholy depraved by unnatural heat or adustion (an obsolete word, meaning scorching). A humor corrupted and blackened by heat was known as "unnatural melancholy," or "melancholy adust."

The term *melancholy* might denote, moreover, the physical and mental condition of the man in whose native temperament black bile was the dominant humor, the man of melancholy complexion. Since this man is cold and dry, he is subject to numerous physical infirmities and to various distressing passions, especially fear and sorrow. His condition, however, is not considered pathological.

There was, further, a form of mental distress called melancholy. This condition differs from the melancholy complexion more in degree than in kind. The principal symptoms are exaggerated griefs and fears, hallucinations, lethargy, unsociability. morbid love of darkness and seclusion, and sometimes bitter misanthropy.

It might seem that since there are so many and such diverse varieties of melancholy, the word could have no definite significance as an exact medical term. In the midst of this diversity, however, one finds the unifying idea of morbid fear and sorrow. A typical Renaissance definition of melancholy by Du Laurens clarifies its meaning: "A kind of dotage without any fever, having for his ordinarie companions feare and sadness, *without apparent occasion.*" (Italics mine.)

What about treatment? The curative measures recommended by the ever-increasing number of medical writers may be roughly divided into cures aimed at the body and cures aimed at the mind.

Evacuation of the offending humor was the most obvious therapeutic measure. This was accomplished by bloodletting. The medical writers name the specific veins to be opened for the evacuation of melancholy from the spleen, the liver, the head, and so forth. The most common method of evacuation was purgation, and black hellebore was the favorite purgative. Clysters and emetics were sometimes recommended.

In addition to these drugs, there were various pharmaceutical concoctions the physician might employ. These included *preparatives*—medicines administered before purgation; *alteratives*—which rendered the humor less noxious by thinning and warming; and *comfortatives*—medicines to cheer up the spirit so that they would warm and enliven the patient's sluggish blood. Some of the prescriptions printed in the medical works are extremely elaborate and complicated, and it would take the physician or apothecary many hours of labor to prepare them.

Thomas Sydenham, who was called the Hippocrates of his day, adjusted his treatment to the special requirements of each case. Not only did he recommend great caution in regard to bleeding and purging, he even refrained completely from their use in cases of physical debilitation. He administered his blood-building remedies with the same caution. He was aware of individual reactions to different medicines and knew that some hypochondriacs had so strong an idiosyncrasy as to feel an absolute repugnance against his "hysterical pills." In such cases, he omitted medications altogether, relying entirely on "the prince and patron of physicians . . . Time."

The medical writers of the age had a great deal to say about the proper diet of the melancholic patient. The dietary directions given by Burton and Du Laurens are typical: the patient should eat plentifully of nourishing food, for fattening is one means of cure. He should drink thin wines of light color and avoid dark wines, especially if they are old.

If possible, the patient should expose himself only to warm, moist air, and his surroundings should be light and cheerful. He should take exercise in moderation, and the physician must see that he does so in such a pleasant place as a garden or meadow. He should bathe often in warm water to warm and moisten his system.

The psychological methods of cure include, first of all, mental diversion. The patient should never be allowed to indulge his penchant for melancholy meditation or to brood over his fancies. Solitary meditation strengthens the hold that melancholy has upon him, and by brooding over his anxieties, he fixed them more firmly in his mind. He should never be left alone. He should be kept busy with something that will keep his thoughts pleasantly engaged. He should hunt, fish, take part in sports, travel, attend plays and pageants, and frequent social gatherings.

Perhaps the best medicine of all was gaiety. In Burton's opinion, nothing is so effective in curing melancholy "as a cup of strong drink, mirth, musick, and merry company." Pleasure not only diverts the mind from melancholic broodings, but also has beneficial physiological effects. Joy is a warm, moist passion and promotes the generation of good blood and spirit to counteract the cold, dry, melancholic humor.

The emotions of the patient must be controlled with great care. He should be scrupulously protected from everything that might frighten or grieve him. If fear or sorrow has been the cause of his malady, he should by no means be allowed to see or hear anything that might remind him of it. His friends should reason with him affably, counsel him, and encourage him. They should offer him consolation for his sorrows, as Timothy Bright, in a prefatory letter, comforts the "Melancholicke friend: M." to whom his treatise on melancholy is addressed.

The patient may do much toward his own cure. He must confide in his friends: "Grief concealed strangles the soul," but when one's sorrow is imparted to a friend, "it is instantly removed by his counsel, wisdom, persuasion, advice." He who wishes to aid a melancholic person cannot confine himself to pharmaceutical and dietary measures; indeed, he may have to intervene in the most intimate affairs of the patient's life.

The subject of melancholic hallucinations deserves some attention, for it introduces us to the area of hypochondriacal case histories. A delusion that lodged itself in a melancholic mind was very tenacious. Melancholic persons were peculiarly subject to hallucinatory obsessions and fixed ideas, usually of a sorrowful and fearful nature. Medical writers of the Renaissance often paused in their more serious business to tell stories about the strange fancies of melancholic men. Many of these stories are repeated over and over, and some are derived from classical sources. When one looks up these sources, however, one finds that some of these tales were not originally told in connection with melancholy. Melancholy seems to have attracted to itself many stories originally associated with other sorts of mental conditions.

Many hypochondriacal persons had absurd anxieties regarding themselves. Some thought they were earthen pots and were continually afraid of being broken; some thought they were urinals. One believed that he was a brick and would not drink for fear of dissolving himself. Another was afraid to sit, because he thought that his buttocks were made of glass; another thought that he had no head; another that he had loathsome sores on his body; another that he was dead. Hypochondriacal persons sometimes imagined that they were birds or other animals and imitated their voices and movements. The grimmest form of hypochondriacal melancholy was lycanthropy, the wolf madness, which constitutes the subject matter of the most lurid chapters in classical, medieval, and Renaissance medical works.

It is not possible to find definite medical explanations for all these various hallucinations. The writers who tell the tales usually throw all cases together into the vague category of melancholic dotages, and tell the stories, one suspects, more for entertainment than for the instruction of their readers. Certain delusions, however, are specifically explained. Du Laurens associates certain fancies with internal physical causes, with a ring of plausibility.

> Such as are of an extreme dry temperature, and have the braine also very dry; if they happen commonly to looke upon some pitcher or glasse . . . they will judge themselves to be pitchers or glasses. Such as are troubled with wormes either in the stomacke or guts, will easily receive, if they are melancholikely disposed, that they have some serpent, viper, or other living thing in their bellies. Such as are troubled with very much windiness, will oftentimes imagine themselves flying in the ayre, and to become birds. They that abound in seede, will runne a madding after women, having the same for continual objects before their eyes.

If the patient was obsessed with an irrational fancy, it was part of the physician's task to dispel it. The mind must be eased before the body can be cured, and in some cases correcting the delusion was alone sufficient for the cure. However, the hypochcndriacal patient was very obstinate and intractable. Any attempt to persuade him that his fancy was groundless only made him cling to it more stubbornly, and anyone who tried to reason with him became the object of his sullen suspicion. The physician, therefore, had to employ a certain psychological strategy. First, he had to win the patient's confidence, and to do so he had to humor him, agree with everything that he said, no matter how preposterous it might have been. "They will give ear to such as will sooth them up," counsels Du Laurens. "If they say they have swallowed frogs, or a snake, by all means grant it, and tell them you can easily cure it, 'tis an ordinary thing." Having established the proper relationship with the patient, the physician then proceeded to combat the delusion, but he had to do so without betraying any skepticism concerning it.

To illustrate, a certain hypochondriac believed that he had an enormous nose, and no one could persuade him otherwise. Finally, a physician "more expert in this humour than the rest" visited him. The doctor showed great astonishment at the size of the patient's nose and thus won his complete confidence. Two or three mock operations, performed while the patient was blindfolded, convinced him that his nose was reduced to normal proportions.

There is the story of a Paris lawyer who thought that he was dead and therefore would not eat. His ingenious nephew dressed himself in a shroud and, garbed as he was as a dead man, ate in the presence of his uncle. In this way, the hypochondriacal lawyer was persuaded that the dead took food as do the living.

A certain gentleman believed that his bones were so soft that they would crumple if he stood up. A clever physician assured him that he could easily cure this infirmity and administered medicines to purge melancholy, representing them as remedies for softness of bone. Thus body and mind were cured at the same time.

Finally, what were the social and cultural attitudes of the English toward melancholy? On the whole, the attitude was one of respect. This was true both in the late sixteenth and early seventeenth centuries, but especially during the latter period when the condition was definitely fashionable. Many English intellectuals, finding something attractive in the melancholic character, caught the malady.

The roll of literary melancholics of the period is rather an impressive one. Sir Philip Sidney, Robert Greene, Thomas Lodge, Thomas Nashe, John Lyly, Francis Bacon, Edmund

Spenser, George Chapman, Nicholas Breton—all these revealed that they suffered from the malady. John Donne's "constant infirmity," one learns from Izaak Walton's biography, was "vapours from the spleen." Donne himself was highly conscious of his affliction: "I languish, prest with Melancholy," and during his critical illness of 1623, he reflected gloomily upon his condition: "But what have I done, either to breed, or to breath these vapours? Did I infuse, did I drinke in Melancholly into my selfe?" And of Robert Burton, it is, of course, widely known that he undertook the composition of his classic *The Anatomy of Melancholy* in order to combat it in himself.

There is no evidence that any of these men of letters rejoiced in their melancholy; in fact, most of them characterized it as a very wretched condition. Yet, they were not ashamed of it; Greene was the only one to apologize for it. Clearly, the Elizabethan intellectual found a certain amount of satisfaction in the idea that he was melancholic.

Several scholars of the Renaissance noted that there was undoubtedly some connection between the vogue of intellectual melancholy and the temper of that age. The late English Renaissance was a period of progressively deepening despondency, and many explanations have been offered for the state of joylessness: social, political, and religious turmoil, intellectual satiety and confusion, loss of faith in man's freedom and preeminence, bewilderment and uncertainty due to the discoveries of the new sciences, and a belief in the senility of nature (what we now call entropy) and the degeneration of man. All of these explanations are partially right, and taken together they probably reflect something approaching the truth.

It is not strange that melancholy should have appealed so strongly to intelligent men in such an era. It seemed to offer an avenue of escape from a disheartening world. The melancholic person could retire within himself and find compensation for the ills of the world in sober, or not so sober, contemplation. And if they did not succeed in escaping from despondency, the concept of melancholy at least defined their state of mind, offered a satisfactory explanation for what was going on within them, and provided them with a respected pattern of conduct.

As Lawrence Babb has pointed out, Elizabethan melancholy began as a fashionable affectation, as an imitation of an Italian and French attitude. Unlike most fads, however, it did not flourish briefly and die. It established itself so firmly in English thought and literature that it persisted for generations. Under new names, the melancholic malady continued to trouble the English until late in the eighteenth century.

The eighteenth century was a period of transition in medicine. Discoveries in pathology did not yet bring about a division of medicine into diseases in which autopsy findings were definite and could be used to explain the symptoms, and diseases in which autopsy findings were vague. Yet the writings of British clinicians of the eighteenth century treated mental and emotional disorders as fully as they discussed conditions belonging in the field of internal medicine. In addition, some physicians devoted entire volumes to the separate considerations of mental diseases, and both Cheyne and Robert Whytt published books on neurotic disorders as such. B. de Mandeville, reverting to an earlier literary form, wrote a book of dialogues between a physician and a middle-aged hypochondriac who was married to a young hysteric. (Did this trio foreshadow the modern urban social unit of husband, wife, and psychiatrist?)

The many different bodily symptoms of neurosis were described in many eighteenth-century works, and most authors specifically mentioned anxiety as a manifestation of the hypochondriacal disorder. While the bodily signs were described more fully, yet the authors indicated that anxiety was an important symptom or, in some cases, the outstanding psychological sign of the syndrome. Cheyne's book, which included descriptions of his own hypochondriacal sufferings, also emphasized the occurrence of ". . . apprehension and remorse . . . a perpetual anxiety and inquietude . . . a melancholy fright and panick where my reason was of no use to me . . ." Whytt, although he mentioned anxiety and other psychological symptoms only briefly, referred to "fearfulness" as a principal symptom and noted "uneasiness not to be described."

The great Philippe Pinel censured English and German writers for vagueness of description and for producing mere compilations intermingled with a few scattered facts. It is true that collection and classification were the main preoccupations of all branches of eighteenth-century learning, yet many treatises on mental disorders do not deserve Pinel's reproaches. In all these writings, anxiety was described as a regularly observed manifestation of hypochondria; moreover, many writers emphasized the severity of the anxiety. Forster stated that "melancholy madness is commonly no more than the hypochondriacal affection aggravated." Similar ideas were expressed by various continental authors; Hoffman, who vigorously emphasized the frequent occurrence of anxiety in melancholy, distinguished between primary melancholy and "symptomatic melancholy from hypochondriacal and hysterical indispositions." Arnold wrote a thorough historical review of anxiety in melancholy, from Hippocrates and Aretaeus onward—a work greatly admired by Dr. Johnson.

To these writers the "constant internal anxiety" was a "principal symptom," "fixed," "habitual," "perpetual," "always personal," "irrational," "delusive," "inexpressible," and "almost unbearable." The mind was "irritable, fickle, and apprehensive"; the patients were "hypped and vapoured with imaginary or trifling evils." The anxiety was always described as attached to some real or imaginary phenomenon. The concept of free-floating anxiety did not appear in eighteenth-century discussions of the symptom, although Macbride suggested that anxiety might be primary: "Anxiety excites the notion of some impending evil."

While basically agreeing on the importance of anxiety in hypochondria, most writers held markedly different beliefs about its causation. Cheyne thought that abnormal viscosity of the blood caused a slowing of all bodily functions and thereby precipitated anxiety. His contemporary, Cadogan, stated that nervousness in general was due to "an acid crudity of our fluids," anticipating modern injunctions to stay on the alkaline side. Others believed that a "driving inward of the humours" was the mechanism.

On the other hand, all authors of the period agreed on the more remote causes of the syndrome. Trauma and bodily constitution were considered of great importance. The role of chronic illness was stressed by Whytt: "There are few chronic distempers in which hypochondria and hysteric symptoms are not more or less blended or intertwined." Climatic conditions were also regarded as important. Cox wrote that certain patients became "a sort of animated barometer," and Cheyne's *Essay on Health and Long Life* stated that some patients began to "sink, droop and languish about Christmas or midwinter . . . those who have very weak nerves, fail sooner, even about the Autumnal Equinox."

References to a great increase in the incidence of disorders of which anxiety is a component are often found in the works cited here. Cheyne noted, inaccurately, that neurotic disorders were virtually unknown to our ancestors, and that almost one-third of all complaints presented by patients in England were of an emotional nature. Several writers noted that nervous disorders were now common among the poor and among country people, and Trotter commented haughtily that "Hypochondria, lowness of spirits and hysterics are now almost as frequent with the more humble, as amongst the higher ranks of society."

The medical writings of the eighteenth century contain references to the contemporary philosophical psychology of Berkeley, Hume, and Hartley. However, this philosophical material proved to be of little value to British clinicians of the period. These men developed their appreciation of the importance of anxiety as a symptom through their own observations and through their study of the ancients. The current belief that anxiety is actually the core of the problem of emotional disorders is the product of a later century and another region. It originated in the intuitive analyses of continental writers and was not a direct outgrowth of the extensive clinical observations of eighteenth-century British physicians.

The idea that sexual drives are an important cause of various mental and emotional disorders has been touted as a discovery of current psychiatry, whereas in fact this idea arose in the remote past. Burton, in discussing melancholy and madness in 1621, said, "Venus omitted produceth like effects," and supported his statement with quotations from the writings of authorities of the two preceding millennia. He referred to the hypochondria of maidens, nuns, and widows in another section of *The Anatomy*, and in still other parts he stated that normal sexual function was important to mental health. His work calls attention to the enormous ancient literature on the presumed role of disturbed sexual functioning in the causation of mental and emotional disorders.

Democritus believed the womb to be the origin of six hundred evils, and Galen declared that sex was the *cause* of both physical and mental disorders. On the other hand, Paulus Aegineta wrote: "The best possible remedy for melancholy is coition. It will restore to reason those who are otherwise afflicted with mania." Avicenna also prescribed sexual activity for the prevention and cure of mental disorders, and a forgotten twelfth-century Frenchman specifically recommended a love affair as a sure cure for megalomania.

In the eighteenth and nineteenth centuries, the growth of systematic psychiatry resulted in extensive clinical inquiries into the causes of all emotional disorders, and it is difficult to find any writer on the subject in this period who did not consider sex important in these conditions. Ryan listed hypochondria, mania, monomania, and other mental disorders as among the consequences of continence. Hippocrates and Actuarius described hysteria—long considered equivalent to hypochondria in men—as most frequently attacking virgins and widows, but Leo thought that it also occurred in men who had been restricted from venery.

Pinel wrote that hysterical manifestations depend almost universally upon some concealed or suppressed exertion of the passions, and others believed that both hypochondria and hys-

teria were due to similar predispositions, but that hysteria was
more commonly due to difficulties involving "the imperious laws
of reproduction," specifically those caused by continence, excessive sexual activity, and the stresses of puberty. An American
psychiatrist observed that nine times out of ten, hysteria arises
from continence, whereas Pierre Briquet, whose *Traité . . .de
l'Hystérie* is one of the great monuments of psychiatry,
minimized the role of sexual factors in hysteria. He was labeled a
prude by his contemporaries.

   With the passage of time, concepts of the nature and
symptoms of the condition broadened. In some ways, this tendency was harmful, because disorders that are clearly not hysterical were included under that heading; on the other hand, it
was beneficial in that it brought about the recognition of the
relationship of hysteria and hypochondria to other neuroses.
Charcot and Pierre Marie explicitly discussed this relationship in
their article on hysteria in Tuke's great *Dictionary of Mental
Disease*. They also stated that the disorder was "less a disease in
the ordinary sense of the word, than a peculiarly constituted
mode of feeling and reaction"—an extraordinarily modern notion.

   Along with the broadening of the concept of the nature of
hysteria/hypochondria, there occurred an increase in the
number of sexual factors that were supposed to cause it. Many
causes were listed, including "imperfect coition, and abstinence
from sexual intercourse," or "forcibly repressed desires, especially sexual." But Pierre Janet was more cautious on the subject:
"Is genital sensibility a center around which other psychological
syntheses are gathered? We do not wish to draw any conclusion."

   As we shall see in the case histories of hypochondria in
chapter 4, very little has changed in the ways physicians view the
role and influence of anxiety and sex in this disorder. The
confusion and disagreements over the matter were greatly aggravated with the arrival of Freudian psychology, although the focus
shifted away from hypochondria toward assessments of anxiety
and sex in other contexts.

The ever-growing interest in hypochondria was fully expressed in the title of a 1729 work by Nicholas Robinson, M.D.: *A New System of the Spleen, Vapours, and Hypochondriack Melancholy wherein all the Decays of the Nerves, and Lownesses of the Spirits are mechanically Accounted for.* This interest, however, was far from being purely medical; poets, playwrights, and writers continued to analyze the malady as they had been doing since antiquity.

The minor eighteenth-century English poets were intensely interested in what they preferred to call "spleen." Among the pre-Romantics are Thomas Gray, whose famous "Elegy" was responsible for the vogue of "graveyard poetry," and Edward Young, whose *Night Thoughts* inspired a whole series of imitative nocturnal lyrics. More to the point is the work of Anne Finch, Countess of Winchilsea, and in particular her remarkable pindaric ode, "The Spleen." So close is this work to a clinical description that when her friend, Dr. W. Stukeley, was prevailed upon to publish his medical lecture, *Of the Spleen,* in 1723, he illustrated it not only with numerous anatomical plates of the dissected organ, but also with a reprint of Anne Finch's entire ode.

The poetess considered both the essence and the causes of spleen inexpressible and limited herself to describing some of its effects, and among the major ones is insomnia.

> On sleep intruding do'st thy shadows spred,
> thy gloomy terrors round the silent bed,
> and croud with boding dreams the melancholy head.

Sleeplessness leaves the mind vulnerable to dreadful visions, the spectral fantasies of spleen, whose results can be catastrophic. Thus, Finch ascribes the defeat of Brutus by Octavian to the nightmares to which the former was subject, and concludes that he was "vanquish'd by the Spleen." Contradicting the prevailing medical opinion, the poetess rejects the idea that spleen can be attributed to physical causes. Rather it is the soul that is "clogged" and thus prevented from continuing to flourish.

There is no remedy. In the penultimate stanza of the poem,

the expression "in vain" recurs five times in as many verses. Music, the traditional palliative, is always either too sweetly sad or too light. The remedies that the apothecaries have concocted, the infusions of "Indian leaf" and the "parch'd eastern berry" are worse than useless. The concluding verses of the poem are addressed to the members of the healing profession, and could hardly be more negative in tone. All the scientific research of the doctors and all their dissections lead not to a cure, not even to a discovery of the roots of the disease, but to the physician's becoming infected with the malady himself. Anne Finch denies the possibility of healing the illness, as well as the existence of physiological causes. When one reads the terminal lines, negating as they do all the vaunted powers of the practitioner's art, one wonders whether Dr. Stukeley understood or even read the poem, although it stands as the foreword to his treatise. In the classical tradition of skepticism toward the medical profession, the poetess mocks not only the incompetence of physicians but their avarice as well:

> Tho' the physician's greatest gains,
> altho' his growing wealth he sees
> daily encreas'd by ladies fees,
> yet do'st thou baffle all his studious pains.

The ode, "The Spleen," is but one of many poems devoted to this topic. In the same genre, the most popular specimen was probably Matthew Green's verse epistle to Mr. Cuthbert Johnson, "The Spleen." In fact, this poem gained such notoriety for its author that he became known as "the Spleen Green." His purpose in composing the work was very different from that of Anne Finch. "I do not mean/to write a treatise on the Spleen," he explains, and goes on to contend that his goal is to provide various methods of driving away the "day-mare Spleen." Green wastes little time on abstractions and hortatory advice. The major part of his poem is given over to a list of dos and don'ts. To counter spleen, one should restrict oneself to a diet of plain food and engage in healthy distractions, including hunting, attendance at the theater and concerts, reading, good conversation and companionship, a modicum of drink and mirth, and sensual pleasures, provided the last is indulged in not too frequently and always in the conjugal bed. The catalog of things to avoid includes gambling, passions, overinvolvement in politics, social climbing, scheming, pride, ambition, anxieties of all sorts, and whimsical behavior. Above all, one should have confidence in God, although mystic excesses and theological inquiries are forbidden. One should follow the poet's example: "I no anxious thoughts bestow/On matters I can never know."

Meanwhile the French were quite aware of "the English malady" and its fashionable aspects, which they did not hesitate to caricature, but for them, in life as well as in art, ennui became the central question of existence. What troubled the French intellectuals deeply was the fact that while they accepted Pascal's premise that ennui is the basis of the human condition, they were unable to come to terms with it. Sensualism and rationalism made it impossible for them to accept the Pascalian solution of faith, but they were at a loss to find something to take its place.

In the hope of hiding the abyss they were unable to fill, Voltaire and his contemporaries had recourse to wit; with it, they thought they could escape their vertigo. When in Beaumarchais's *Barber of Seville,* the Count Almaviva asks Figaro how he could maintain his cheerfulness in the face of so much adversity, the resourceful valet replies, "I hasten to laugh, for fear of having to weep." Nevertheless, wit provided little protection from ennui as it was primarily the hallmark of eighteenth-century salons, where wit was regarded as the highest of virtues.

If there was a major literary figure of this period who was untouched by ennui, it was Diderot. Perhaps because his own immunity gave him a degree of objectivity, Diderot was able to describe the state lucidly. Consciously keeping it at a distance by emphasizing its foreignness and making his reader an accomplice in ignorance, he begins a letter to Sophie Volland by admitting his own lack of knowledge of the subject: "You have no idea of what is meant by the spleen, or English vapors; I didn't either." He goes on to explain that in order to inform himself about this malady, he has asked one of its victims, their mutual Scottish friend Hoop, to describe it for him. The next portion of the letter consists of his transcription of Hoop's actual words:

> "I have been subject to a general malaise of an annoying nature for twenty years now. My head is never free of it. Sometimes it is so heavy that it is like a weight pulling me forward, which might hurl me from a window into the street, or to the bottom of a river, if I were standing on its edge. My thoughts are somber, and I am consumed by sorrow and ennui. Are you familiar with the sort of stupor that one feels after having slept too long? That is my usual state; I am disgusted with life. The slightest changes in the weather are violent jolts for me, and I am unable to stay in one place. I am completely out of tune with others; I like what they dislike, and dislike what they like. There are days when I hate light, and my nights are agitated by a thousand bizarre dreams. I have never known such despair; I feel old, decrepit, impotent. . . ."

Most elements of ennui that we have previously discussed are to be found in this passage: depression that can lead to suicide, the lack of will that characterizes lethargy, an inward restlessness, a hatred of life, hypersensitivity, insomnia, and spiritual and physical impotence. This combination of symptoms is the "usual state" in which the victim of ennui lives.

Rather than commenting on Hoop's malady, Diderot ends his letter with a description of his own ordinary state. It is one that exudes such a sense of well-being that any form of ennui would be impossible to experience. He feels as comfortable in his life as he did in the old bathrobe to which he had devoted one of his most eloquent eulogies. He is at home in a world that shelters him from ennui.

In nineteenth-century literature, both English and continental, Chateaubriand's René has become the prototype of the romantic protagonist destroyed by ennui. René, in a sense, is a composite of all his predecessors and a model for all his descendants. The ineffable melancholy with which he is afflicted tinges his entire being:

> I am bored with life; ennui has always consumed me. What interests others does not concern me in the slightest. Shepherd or king, what would I have done with my crook or crown? I would have tired as quickly of glory as of genius, of work as of leisure, of prosperity as of adversity. In Europe and in America, society and nature fatigued me. I am virtuous without pleasure; if I were a criminal I would be one without remorse. What I would like is never to have been born or ever to be forgotten.

René has many descendants in literature, such as Lafcadio in Gide's *The Cellars of the Vatican,* who risks his life to save a girl he does not even know from a burning house, and later kills a perfect stranger by pushing him out of a moving train. His heroic deed was done without pleasure, the senseless murder without remorse. But not even Lafcadio went as far toward total despair as had the exiled René who longed for nothing but the nothingness of never having existed.

In Sénancour's *Obermann,* ennui is no longer considered simply as a menacing danger. Sénancour abandons the clichés of the malady and ceases to seek facile remedies for a complex condition to concentrate on a deep form of ennui that provides the basis for a negative form of mysticism. He dispenses even with the semblance of fiction in *Obermann,* which doesn't even have a shadow of a plot. It consists of a series of letters, written over a period of five years, that Obermann sends to a friend, and they contain almost no external events. Obermann withdraws from society in order to study himself and presents the model of hypochondriacal concentration on his mental state. His debility is such that he cannot even make a minimal effort. His various projects for distracting himself, ranging from that of becoming a writer to the measuring of a decade of rainfall, are all abandoned in their early stages. His existence is of such a tenuous nature that one has the feeling that he will gradually fade away to become a part of the nothingness that haunts him. In structure as well as in its subject matter, *Obermann* is the forerunner of Beckett's equally eventless *Endgame*. In *Endgame*, too, everything gradually runs out; the cookies for Nagg and Nell, the pain-killer for Hamm. Time, too, is running out, for there is no one to rewind the clock that keeps everything going.

The abstract theory of ennui posed by Sénancour was given reality in Flaubert's *Madame Bovary*. Emma was disenchanted early in life, even before her marriage. She "considered herself as being highly disillusioned, having nothing to learn any more, unable to feel anything any more." The images that Flaubert employs to describe her condition have a domestic quality that makes them all the more sinister: "Her life was as cold as an attic whose garret window faces north, and ennui, a silent spider, spun its web in the shadows, in all the corners of her heart." This middle-class ennui is more virulent than the sublime ennui of the allegorical Lélia of George Sand, more deadly even than the arsenic with which Emma kills herself. Its mortal influence continues long after she is laid to rest as Charles Bovary wastes away, as if Emma had infected him with her ennui. In Flaubert's words, "She corrupted him from beyond the tomb." Flaubert's entire work can be seen as a panorama embracing the ennui of the past in *November*, that of the present in *Madame Bovary* and *The Sentimental Education*, and that of the future in *Bouvard and Pécuchet*, his last, unfinished novel.

It is not possible to summarize the intellectual adventure of the confrontation with ennui in the nineteenth century, or even to trace a coherent development or a consistent pattern. Even the philosophers of the age are of no help, for they, too, present us with a wide range of views, running the gamut from Schopenhauer's pessimism to the religious anguish of Kierkegaard. Emile Montégut, a perceptive critic, whose life-span covered most of the century, gives us a clue to a possible unifying factor in a curious fictional essay, "Les confidences d'un hypocondriaque." Most of the work is given over to a confession that an anonymous victim of ennui makes to the author. This hypochondriac has no illusions of grandeur; he will never write a

René or a *Madame Bovary,* and his affliction is in no way a pose. In ennui, of which his friends would like to cure him, he has found a profound sense of beatitude. He has found joy, because he discovered what Obermann had searched for in vain, "the plenitude of nothingness." The only effort that he is still willing to make is his fierce opposition to any attempt to rescue him from his state of blissful inaction, and even this opposition is pure passivity. The author, having heard and recorded the confession, concludes:

> Ennui is no longer a state of unease, as it was in the time of Rousseau, but a state of negation. . . . In this age, everything is receding, everything is becoming sallow and corrupt, even despair, even ennui. . . . The human spirit now derives happiness from its own impotence and places its supreme hope and final recompense in nothingness.

In the twentieth century, ennui is no longer one theme among others, but the dominant one, and intrudes into the works of most contemporary writers. It has been pushed to its extreme limits, and all variations on the theme are exaggerated versions of past experiences. The ancient concept of the melancholic artist is transformed by Proust, who based his entire aesthetics on ennui and erected the monument of *Remembrance of Things Past* in a wasteland later described by T. S. Eliot. The nostalgic sorrow of Verlaine is distilled into the bittersweet poison of F. Scott Fitzgerald. The ennui-inspired sadomasochistic aberrations of René have become the norm, and the twentieth century has made the Marquis de Sade and Sacher-Masoch its patron saints. In the inhuman world of Robbe-Grillet, only structures and objects remain. Ennui is no longer an emotion, but a state of being in which only things and forms can survive. There has been a parallel transformation of metaphors used to describe a world dominated by ennui. For the desert fathers, the world was a desert or cave; in the literature of the twentieth century, the world is a sanatorium, an inverted cylinder, a dead and decaying parish.

To sum up this necessarily cursory literary-historical review of ennui/spleen/melancholy, we have tried to show that excessive preoccupation with one's mental state, that is, mental hypochondria, has always been an important component in our psychological makeup. Moreover, it must not even be regarded as a primarily negative component; it is a state that, if it does not render one sterile, if it does not engulf its victim, can and often does induce efforts to fill the void. It precedes and makes possible artistic creation in the realms of the practical, the spiritual, and the aesthetic. It can cause the melancholy that characterizes the extraordinary man depicted in Aristotle's *Problemata Physica*, it can create the "dark night of the soul" that the mystics had to traverse to find God, and it can be the muse that inspires a poet or a Robert Burton to fill with his song or scholarship the emptiness it had uncovered.

IV. HISTORIES:
Fifty Hypochondriacs

*Some are unhappy through
illness, some are ill through
unhappiness.*

—*Sir Walter Langdon Brown*

The following collection of histories of hypochondriacs was
gleaned from files of psychiatrists, psychotherapists, general
practitioners, and other professionals who have had occasion to
treat, even to cure, patients with hypochondriacal symptoms.
(The commentaries that follow the histories represent the views
and opinions of this writer only. Some readers at least will come
to different conclusions.) Many hypochondriacs were interviewed in person, although many more could not be, and these
interviews were invaluable. Close observation of anguish is more
revealing than studying an account of it.

It is hoped that these histories will succeed in accomplishing
what no amount of exposition and analysis can. It will bring to
life, make vivid for the reader, as it did for the writer, the
sufferings of scores of hypochondriacs; these children, men, and
women, of various backgrounds, occupations, and personalities,
some creative and successful, others paralyzed by anguish, may,
after all, have nothing in common but their sufferings.

Childhood and Adolescent Hypochondria

A tall boy of fifteen complained of "funny spells" in which he
became dizzy, saw black specks and had stomachaches so severe

that they doubled him up. Medical examination revealed no organic illness.

History revealed that at age three he became terrified as he was looking for his mother all over the house from which she had just been rushed to the hospital, where she subsequently died. A year after his mother's death, he saw a horse killed and became hysterical. At age eight, his dog was run over and killed in his sight. He carried the dead dog around, crying, "Now I have nothing left to love me . . ." He lay awake for long periods at night, fearing he was about to die.

This case would have been diagnosed as thanatophobia had it not been for the boy's physical symptoms, which constituted secondary hypochondria. The pediatrician, who treated the boy, used plain, simple counseling with the warm cooperation of the boy's grandmother. The boy was encouraged systematically for every little success, given a chance to earn money and take on responsibilities. His spells gradually became less frequent and intense, and in two years' time he was free of all physical symptoms.

A sweet, attractive little girl of ten complained that she "didn't feel well," and felt as if she were dead and said that "things aren't real." She said she worried over her mother's health and was afraid she would have to go to the hospital and never come back. She was terrified over her father's illness, which was in fact indigestion, and her mother was in good health. According to the child, he had "rocks in his liver," "can't sleep because his heart hurts so, groans something awful, gets mother up, and his heart makes noises like a cat meowing." She felt that a kidnapper was going to come in her window, take her to the basement and keep her tied up, with a stream of water dropping on her forehead. Her dreams were full of grotesque images, bright dots "going around and around everything," and many colors moving in and out.

It turned out that her mother had been in the habit of taking her to funerals and showing her the dead in their coffins since she was four years old. The girl "got real dizzy" when she thought how sick her father and mother were and how they would look in their coffins. In school, she sometimes felt that her hand and foot didn't belong to her.

The pediatrician in charge of this case engaged the parents' cooperation. The father explained to the child the true nature of his physical complaints and made light of them, while the mother ceased the practice of taking the girl to funerals. The child was quick to grasp the facts, and her symptoms showed immediate improvement. Here, again, the diagnosis is thanatophobia with secondary hypochondria in the form of self-estrangement and delusions.

A plump, dainty little girl of nine complained of dizziness, fainting, and choking. Soon after, she began to refuse to eat or sleep and lost ten pounds in a month. Medical examination showed nothing organically wrong.

History-taking revealed that the child had lived the sheltered life of the well-to-do, petted and loved by both parents, until her mother's controlled social drinking turned into severe alcoholism of such magnitude that she was drunk practically all the time and yelled and cursed. The contrast with her former delightful, loving self was more than the child could bear. One day the child put all her fingers in her mouth, saying that she had poisoned herself, and fainted. Another time, she choked, insisting she had swallowed a chicken bone, and would not eat for three days. She had frequent choking spells and claimed that she had swallowed cotton or metal objects. If she woke up during the night, she ran to the mother's bed, grabbed her, and cried that she was scared. Her latest idea was to wash her hands dozens of times a day until they became chapped and sore and she'd refuse to touch anything.

The father took the girl to a child psychologist. The first therapeutic measure was to keep the mother sober as long as possible, with the ultimate goal of curing her alcoholism. This was successful for a period of four months, during which the child's appetite returned and her other symptoms cleared up promptly. Unfortunately, the mother resumed her drinking, the family moved, and the girl's condition was lost to follow-up. The case was one of primary hypochondria, where the symptoms mimicked the mother's drinking; chances are that this particular childhood hypochondria turned into a chronic one.

A pretty girl of fourteen, apparently nervous, complained of convulsions, heart trouble, and indigestion, which she claimed to have had for three years. Medical examination failed to confirm any of the symptoms. She also added sinking spells, headaches, and anorexia to her complaints.

It turned out that this girl had a low IQ, which prevented her from doing her schoolwork satisfactorily, yet she was promoted each year. Finally, she reached the point where she couldn't stand not being able to do what her classmates were doing. "I am nothing but a fool at school," she burst out. "I can't open my mouth without making a fool of myself." All the complaints were caused by her school situation, and she became nonsocial and phobic.

The school physician assessed the girl's condition correctly and arranged for her to be placed in a special class that matched her abilities. She had no further complaints in the next three years and was free of symptoms upon graduation. This was a case of primary hypochondria brought on by sociocultural factors. Had it not been for the school physican's accurate diagnosis, it could easily have turned into a lifelong hypochondria.

A timid boy of twelve with a high IQ complained of being faint, dizzy, not hearing well, bad headaches, and stomach pains so severe that he had to "lie down and take Alka-Seltzer." "Something squeezes inside my head," he said, and listed pains in his hands, legs, and back. Physical examination offered no clinical proof of any symptom.

Further inquiry revealed that the boy was the only child of a hard-drinking sometime steelworker and a neurotic mother who had always wanted a girl. They all lived in one room with a closet-sized space for cooking. The father despised the boy as a "sissy," while the mother applied rouge and lipstick to his face and taught him to dance, sew, and embroider. At school, the boys, too, called him a "sissy," and his teacher called him stupid in a loud voice, in the presence of a social worker.

The social worker called the boy to the attention of the school psychologist, and they deemed the case hopeless at first.

Then, acting as a team, they undertook the difficult task of counseling the parents. They succeeded in persuading the "he-man" father to teach the boy sports, which would give him prestige with his schoolmates. They also managed to get the father to find a job that suited his skills and the family moved into a three-room apartment with a porch. The mother tearfully agreed to stop treating him as a girl and concentrate on trying for another child. The school principal moved the boy to another class with a kind, understanding teacher, and he became an outstanding student and good at sports. All his symptoms vanished, and his success in school brought parental approval.

This case of primary hypochondria, while apparently successfully treated, seems to be in limbo. The father's penchant for drink, the possible failure of the mother to have a baby girl, and other factors may conspire to bring the original conditions into play again, which may reactivate the hypochondria. There is also the possibility of the boy's becoming homosexual, as the family constellation is classically conducive to its development.

A boy of nine complained of very blurred vision and inability to see the words in his schoolbooks. He said his muscles jerked, his hands shook, he had headaches, pains in the belly, and his "heart goes off like an alarm clock." Medical examination showed normal eyesight and no clinical signs of illness.

The boy's parents regarded him as perfect, until he proved unable to learn to read in first grade. After that, he was scolded, called dumb and stupid, and scorned in comparison with a younger cousin and playmates, who could read well. In school, too, he was ridiculed and taunted. Eventually, he came to be regarded as a family disgrace and a complete failure in school.

No treatment was provided in this case, and when interviewed at age twelve, the boy would not admit that he couldn't read perfectly. His hypochondria was by then deeply rooted, and there was no indication of change in his situation at home or school. Except for the possibility of effective outside intervention, both the hypochondria and the learning disability seemed certain to become entrenched.

A boy of seven with a high IQ complained of severe headaches, frequent vomiting, breaking out in a sweat, turning pale, and feeling that if he did too much, he would "feel sick and faint." Physical examination was negative.

The father turned out to be a bad-tempered, hard-drinking truck driver who beat the boy and the mother frequently. Although recently divorced from the mother, he came to visit every week, never failing to knock mother and son about. The school complained that the boy was not performing at the level of his intelligence and couldn't sit still for a minute. His psychological symptoms included nail-biting, nightmares, and anorexia.

There were routine bureaucratic efforts by the school psychologist to help the boy, but they were neither effective nor persistent. However, when the boy was nine, the mother remarried. The stepfather proved to be understanding and affectionate, and visits from the father ended. The boy gained six pounds in two months, and all his symptoms disappeared. This was a case of primary hypochondria, healed by a sudden improvement in the victim's family situation.

A boy of thirteen complained of dull heart pains, for which he had to "lie down like mother," vomiting spells, and fainting. The symptoms were so long-standing that neither the boy nor the parents could remember when they had begun. Medical examination was negative.

There had been much dissension between the parents ever since the boy was a baby. The mother had long ago turned away from the father and made the boy the sole outlet for her emotions. Her eyes filled with tears, her lips, even her chin, trembled as she talked about her fears for his health. She asked the boy several times a day how he was feeling, and fussed over eating and sleeping habits or anything having to do with health. She had always kept him close, away from his peers.

Aside from his physical symptoms, the boy was full of fears, especially fear of dying, and his schoolmates called him "scaredy-cat." By the time his condition was discovered at thirteen, he preferred to stay close to mother and would have an attack every time he had to go somewhere.

The parents cooperated with the school psychologist to the extent that the mother promised to cease talking about health and showing excessive concern for the boy and the father agreed to spend more time with him. The boy spent more time with his peers, too, and his heart complaints ceased. However, his vomiting spells continued, although less frequently, as the dissension between the parents remained fundamental. This is a classic example of primary hypochondria in males, and the prognosis for the boy cannot be regarded as promising beyond the short term. It is all too likely that the mother's change of attitude will be temporary and superficial, and that the father's interest will wane. Again, the possibility of future homosexuality is present.

A thin, anxious second-generation Japanese girl of fourteen told the school physician that her "nose is spreading out," that she could not get her breath, could not eat, and felt itchy. Physical examination was negative.

The girl's late father had been an Oxford graduate, and the mother and grown-up siblings insisted on high standards. The girl had more and more trouble keeping up at school, as she also had to take piano lessons and attend Japanese school in the evening. Although the family did not punish her, they were very anxious that she keep up the family standards and exerted constant pressure in that regard. Her only recreation was the park or beach once a week.

Her psychological symptoms included crying spells, irritability, insomnia, and fear of the dark.

Her family cooperated to the extent of letting her give up piano lessons, and spend less time on schoolwork, but the Japanese school remained a must. Four months later, the girl was feeling better, but here, again, improvement is likely to be temporary. Maintaining family standards is a long-standing tradition in Japanese culture, and, while outside sociocultural pressures may prevail temporarily, the tradition is too deeply ingrained to be subject to permanent intervention. Interestingly, fifty years ago, the diagnosis would probably have been hysteria in this case.

A thirteen-year-old boy complained dejectedly, "I've got a stiff bone in my head," and, "I can't feel my bowels moving around anymore." He added headaches, dizziness, double vision, and ill-defined abdominal pains. He was pale, stooped, nervous, and malnourished, yet proved to be clinically healthy upon examination.

The boy had been the family favorite until age six, when a baby sister replaced him in that role. At that point, he became closely attached to his older sister, but she died of TB four years later. Shortly after, the school doctor took longer than usual in examining him and made some whispered remarks about his lungs to the nurse. Greatly worried, he began developing all of his late sister's symptoms of TB, which continued for three years. He became very sensitive, cried easily, ate poorly, began to avoid other children, became very forgetful, and lay awake at night waiting to die.

The family doctor gave him a physical examination purely for reassurance, and the negative results of the TB test were shown to the boy for the same reason. The family became very cooperative and supportive, careful to avoid all talk of illness. They invited other boys to their home, and got him occupied with sports and other activities. He gained weight and had no further physical complaints. This is a classic case of hypochondria caused by replacement as favorite child, but reinforced not only by the experience of death of a loved one, but also iatrogenically by the school physician. Fortunately, the wisdom of the family physician became the decisive factor for the time being. The reader should be reminded that this type of childhood experience may, in later life, be triggered by internal or external pressures to reactivate the hypochondriacal condition.

A ten-year-old boy complained of vomiting spells and tics of increasing severity of two years' standing. Physical findings were negative, except for extreme nervousness and malnutrition.

He was an overprotected only son. The mother had hyperthyroidism and the father had had a nervous breakdown; the grandmother was the dominant figure in the family. Each time the boy left the house, the grandmother warned him not to get into cars with men who offered him candy as it might be poisoned or make him unconscious. Also, the grandmother was a fan of crime movies and of anything having to do with crime, fictitious or real. She was in the habit of taking the boy with her when she went to the movies, and there was continual talk about crime stories in the house. The boy was in a constant, pitiful state of nervousness, biting his nails, blinking, grimacing, and twitching.

This case shows the extreme vulnerability of children to pathogenic family influences. All that needed to be done was to counsel the grandmother to stop taking the boy to the movies, and stop talking about crime stories in front of him. As a result of her cooperation, the boy's symptoms disappeared within a month. Nevertheless, the long-term outcome of this case must be placed in doubt.

A girl of sixteen was referred to a psychoanalyst, because of numerous complaints of abdominal pain and of deafness, despite the absence of physical findings.

History revealed consistent exposure to numerous family illnesses, including her own mastoidectomy and appendectomy. She had constant contact with hospitals, both as a visitor and as a patient. Her mother was oversolicitous about health, and the girl was strongly attached to her father, who had numerous gastric complaints. She had suffered from fears of convulsions, death, and later of sexual attacks, since early childhood.

The girl underwent psychoanalysis for a year and a half and gained many insights about her family situation. This produced an easement of her hypochondriacal symptoms, but she was not entirely free of them when analysis stopped. In view of the presence of the numerous factors conducive to hypochondria, chances are that her symptoms became chronic in adulthood.

A boy of seven was referred to a psychotherapist because of his inordinate interest in intestines. His earliest memory was that of a mastoid operation.

Therapy revealed a strong attachment to an oversolicitous mother who prevented social contact with other children. She wouldn't kiss the child for "hygienic reasons," and complained constantly of "nervous" symptoms. The father had an atrophied hand, and the older brother was much interested in ailments of all sorts. The boy had frequent contact with hospitals during the long illness and eventual death of an aunt.

Again, causative factors of hypochondria were numerous in this case, indicating that the boy would grow up to be a hypochondriacal adult. Psychotherapy lasted for fifteen months, but the therapist focused mainly on sexual connections. She related the boy's interest in intestines to sexual curiosity and "incestuous" fantasies about the mother, and to overt fears of castration and death. At the end of therapy, the boy's condition was fundamentally unchanged.

A boy of twelve was referred to a Freudian psychoanalyst on account of his excessive interest in illnesses and body sensations, accompanied by constant physical complaints. He had had a tonsillectomy at three, circumcision at six, measles at nine, mumps at eleven, and chronic bronchitis at eleven and a half. "I am a lung case," he announced proudly.

Until age six, he was brought up by a grandmother who was unduly solicitous about illness and then by the mother who was also much concerned about health, yet distinctly hostile to the boy. The stepfather frequently urged the mother to go to bed because of her fatigue and overexcitability. Between ages six and eight, the boy lived next door to a psychiatric hospital; he often crawled through a fence and had frequent contacts with patients.

The boy had been in analysis a year and a half when his case history was taken, and his condition was unchanged. It is difficult to foresee favorable progress as his family situation remains bleak.

A boy of fourteen was referred to the school psychologist for rebellious behavior, but it turned out that he demonstrated a wide variety of hypochondriacal symptoms. He complained of fatigue, headaches, dizziness, lack of vitality, fear of hernia, various abdominal symptoms, and fear of appendicitis.

His medical history showed delay in walking, delay in speech, measles and mumps before age four, operation for removal of an object from his larynx, and removal of tonsils and adenoids at four and a half.

The mother could not endure the sight of blood, which served as her excuse for not accompanying the boy to the hospital for his operations. The boy was very hostile toward the father, who was consistently derogatory to him, and he was very competitive with his younger brother.

The boy had great difficulty in sexual adjustment, and failed to develop a sex role by the age of fourteen. He liked to masquerade on the telephone as a girl, successfully using a girl's voice, and made, but never kept, dates with men. He had had no sexual contact with girls, and expressed frank envy of women.

The school psychologist's records made much of the fact that the boy masturbated every day, which was followed by fatigue, headache, and dizziness, and she spent considerable time on persuading the boy to abandon the practice. The hypochondriacal components of the boy's condition received no attention beyond being noted. After only three interviews, the boy's family moved to another city, and nothing further is known about him. He was clearly in the throes of a complex neurotic, perhaps even psychotic, condition, to which the hypochondria was secondary.

Interviewed at age thirty, a male businessman, who stated that he is no longer a hypochondriac, recalled his childhood hypochondria. His father was very robust and made much of his excellent health; the phrase, "I've never spent a single day in sickbed," was used often. When the boy was thirteen, the father died suddenly of a heart attack. The mother was extremely illness-conscious, and, though seldom ill, she complained a great deal about undefined aches and pains.

At age six, the boy developed the belief that there was a hole in his neck. He avoided mirrors and kept a hand over the imagined hole whenever he was not alone. He kept this belief to himself, never confiding in family or friends.

About a year later, he was taken to a pediatrician at a nearby

medical center for a general checkup, and, much to his own sur-
prise, he told the doctor about the hole in his neck. The doctor,
neither making fun of him nor patronizing him, succeeded in dispel-
ling the delusion by patiently explaining to the boy that people do
sometimes imagine that there is something wrong with them when
there is not. The boy believed him, because he had always liked and
trusted him.

After that, until about age twenty, the boy suffered a variety of
hypochondriacal conditions, all of them related to the neck, exterior
and interior. The doctor he had trusted died when the boy was about
eleven, and he never spoke of his neck problems to anybody. The
condition disappeared spontaneously, but, curiously, the boy, and
later the man, never trusted another doctor. Also, it was noted
during the interview that from time to time he touched an area of his
neck, apparently unaware of doing so. In passing, he referred to the
fact that his adolescent daughter was a hypochondriac.

This clearly could be the incomplete story of a closet hypochondriac, and, while one can only speculate, the confession of past
hypochondria may be a cover-up for a present, secret one. The
daughter's hypochondria is a clue to the probability that she has
picked up and followed the scent of her father's condition. As is
generally the case with closet hypochondriacs, this man gives no
indication of suffering, and apparently leads the life of a successful, healthy businessman.

Are there any common denominators to be found in cases of
childhood and adolescent hypochondria? The following observations seem justifiable:

1. There was exposure in early life to numerous complaints and
   evidence of illnesses, invalidism, life-threatening experiences of various sorts, or death, of close family members.
2. There is likely to have been actual experience of frequent
   illness, contacts with physicians, numerous physical examinations, or life-threatening episodes.
3. There is likely to have been strong identification with an ill

person, or one who exaggerated body sensations, which provided a model for a milieu of illness.

Adult Hypochondriacs as Patients and Outpatients at Hospitals and Clinics

A thirty-two-year-old married steelworker went to the outpatient department of a London hospital complaining of attacks of palpitations, breathlessness, and fear, usually after meals. He had had his first attack two years earlier, after breakfast, in a setting to which he could not attach any particular significance. The attacks lasted from ten minutes to four hours.

He had visited many private practitioners before his appearance at the hospital and received a wide variety of medications, one of which resulted in skin eruptions from overdoses of bromides. None of the prescriptions brought any relief, and they represented considerable expense to him. He eventually devised his own diet, consisting only of milk, eggs, bread, and one orange per day and had lost thirty pounds during the previous six months.

His symptoms became worse after his wife had a baby following a difficult delivery, yet he remained at work throughout this period. All physical examinations, including one at the hospital, were negative, and while he believed that his condition was not due to a physical illness, he was yet unable to be reassured by his negative physical examinations.

His personal history revealed that his father died when he was five, and after the age of seven he was brought up by his maternal grandparents. As a child he was spoiled by his grandmother, but she continually threatened him with a tonsil operation and he developed an intense fear of all operations. When he was actually taken to a hospital for a tonsillectomy at age twelve, he ran away.

His marriage had been successful and his wife was greatly worried about his condition, but they had not had sexual relations since the birth of their child, because she feared another pregnancy and his sexual desire had also ceased.

On his second visit, he was urged to give more information about his history. After much hesitation, he said that his first attack occurred the morning after he had attended a lecture where he had seen a film of an operation on cancer of the stomach. He had not seen a film of any kind since then, and he volunteered the information that his grandmother had died of cancer nine years before. "I remember how my grandmother would have these spells," he said. "Maybe I have inherited the condition."

This was a very interesting case where hypochondria served as a cover-up, a substitute, for cancer phobia, as the astute physician attending him at the hospital immediately realized. The patient had put himself on an anticancer diet to the point of starvation. He was instructed to stop taking any medication and return at once to a normal diet. He was also told to keep reassuring himself that these attacks could not possibly hurt him, because they were the result of his fear of cancer, which he now realized was unfounded, and that they would soon cease. The attacks indeed ceased almost immediately, and he regained his original weight in a matter of months.

A thirty-three-year-old housewife was admitted to a hospital with a ten-year history of body complaints, which for the past two years had kept her in bed and caused her to take sedatives every day. Her complaints of backache, headache, stomachache, insomnia, amenorrhea, "pulling and drawing in my womb," restlessness, choking feelings, and hot flushes had led her through a great variety of medical treatments, including two operations. On admission to the hospital she was disheveled, restless, and agitated.

"I have a headache most of the time; my eyes ache. Everything I eat rolls over and over. My abdomen swells up. I can't bear to be on my feet." Her essential complaint was: "My female organs aren't functioning at all. When I don't menstruate, my blood all rushes to my head. My female organs are all gone."

Gynecologic examination showed nothing to account for her symptoms, nor did a general physical checkup.

History-taking revealed that both her parents died when she was four, and she was sent to the farm of her grandfather who, she claimed, assaulted her sexually when she was about twelve. At thirteen, she was moved to the strict, religious home of an aunt, where she stayed until marriage at twenty. She was often absent from school with complaints of stomachache, and on one occasion she stayed in bed for three months after a case of influenza.

She married in order to have her own home and more freedom, but her husband turned out to be even stricter than her aunt had been. Two years after marriage, having experienced painful and frequent intercourse along with frigidity and fear of pregnancy, she began complaining of gas, a gnawing feeling in her stomach, and choking sensations. At the same time, her periods became irregular, occurring every two or three months, and they were scanty.

During the next two years, she had a tonsillectomy and an appendectomy, and had her left ovary removed, all without relief. One doctor treated her with hormones, and her periods became regular for four months, only to relapse to their previous state. Her husband then sent her to a doctor to cure her frigidity; he treated her with hormone injections, and, she claimed, attempted to assault her. Since then, she has spent most of her time in bed. She said she felt as if she were about to menstruate all the time, and believed that nothing would help her but the removal of all her female organs.

During her first ten days in the hospital, sedatives were gradually withdrawn, despite her clamorous protests, and nurses were told to ignore her complaints. Her agitation was treated with tranquilizers. She remained in the hospital for an entire month and improved considerably. She gained weight and was active with the other patients. Nevertheless, she had no period during her stay and her complaints persisted upon discharge.

This is a case of diffuse hypochondria, and it cannot be said that appropriate treatment was given. According to the hospital records, she was advised upon discharge to develop outside interests and to control her complaints and tell no one about them. It is not very likely that the advice was successfully followed for any length of time. Her hypochondria appears to be based on her fear of sex and serves the practical purpose of enabling her to avoid sexual intercourse with her husband.

A fifty-four-year-old female outpatient complained of abdominal discomfort, backache, vision difficulty, tightness in the throat, and exhaustion when doing housework. "My stomach has fallen, my eyes give me trouble. I have a shooting pain under the arm."

She had been much pampered and babied in early life and readily treated as an invalid. She had had a love affair at nineteen, but her lover died. She married without love at twenty-four and developed frigidity and dyspareunia (pain during intercourse). She had two difficult labors, and her hypochondria developed after the second one.

She was very interested in medicine and her complaints, and seemed quite content with her hypochondria. She had absolutely no desire to lose her symptoms and had no anxiety about them at all. She visited the clinic three times, but nothing could be done for her. According to reports, six months later she lapsed into chronic invalidism.

The roots of this hypochondria lay in early childhood and came to flower as a result of unfortunate circumstances in later life. As in the preceding case, it also served the purpose of avoiding unwanted intercourse.

A forty-one-year-old man served two years in Vietnam; he saw no combat and spent the time guarding prisoners, an experience he quite enjoyed. While in Vietnam he had an accident, but had no ill effects from it. Upon discharge he began receiving monthly service-connected compensation payments, and it was then that he started complaining of indigestion, restlessness, and insomnia. He could find no work, but he visited numerous doctors and clinics and lived off relatives and his monthly checks. In the next five years, he started at fifty different jobs, leaving them after a few days due to his indigestion.

He was the fifth child in a family of ten. One brother had epilepsy, but there was no other medical history. His father was a bully who made much fun of him. At fifteen, he went to work as a tailor's presser, at which he worked on and off, earning very little, until he joined the Army. He seemed selfish, irritable, dishonest, and lazy, and had few friends. His sex life consisted of regular masturbation and prostitutes once a month.

He went to the clinic to get support for his application for increased compensation payments. He complained of belching and pain in the stomach and chest. "I guess it's heart trouble. The doctors can't get to the root of it." Examination revealed nothing, and he was much aggrieved and self-pitying. He could be aroused to petulant and noisy indignation when questioned about his illness. He was typical of the "flatulent windy melancholy," described by Burton.

The man obviously did not want to be relieved of his complaints, but only desired compensation for them. He was quite uncooperative in any attempt to explain them, left without improvement, and did not return.

This was a very purposive type of hypochondria, which gained for the patient the support of his relatives and money from the government. It seems almost like a case of malingering, but is, in fact, a hypochondria that serves as compensation for the patient's lack of accomplishments and is rooted in the dependency relationship with the compensation payments, which actually produced the condition.

A married twenty-five-year-old woman complained of diffuse pains all over her body, and a heavy feeling in her head, which, she felt, might be a tumor like one of her friends had. "My heart feels big and heavy. It quivers. I feel smothery and choked in the throat." She was not at all upset by any of these symptoms, but she would not accept any suggestion that her complaints were not physical.

She was pampered as a child and allowed to stay home from school with any minor bodily complaint. She went to work in a laundry and continued to have bodily complaints, which often resulted in getting time off. She took barbiturates in abundant quantities. She had two unwanted children by Caesarean section, and after the second one she claimed to be unable to do any work. She has left all housework to her husband, whom she tyrannized by means of her illness.

This is another case of purposive hypochondria, although it originated in childhood. She has learned to utilize invalidism, and her increase in symptoms may be even due to barbiturates. She obviously doesn't want to change. She was told at the clinic that she was strong enough to work, but it is quite unlikely to have had any effect.

A thirty-three-year-old happily married machinist with five children complained at a clinic about numbness of the temples and a lump in the throat. "Makes my throat raw; my eyes feel like they are expanding. So tired in the chest. Every nerve in my body twittering. Gas in the stomach feels like it works up to the temples. I feel like the skin on my face is all drawn up."

His family history showed nothing medically significant, except that his brother was sent to a state hospital with paranoiac schizophrenia three years earlier, which coincided with the beginning of the hypochondriacal symptoms. The patient was not certain that the brother's diagnosis was justified, and even if it was, he felt bad about his being in a state hospital.

He did not seem upset in relating his symptoms; his face was consistently blank. He was told that his physical condition was excellent and that he should continue all his activities, because his symptoms would diminish. He went back to the clinic once a week and improved steadily as various areas of his life were discussed. The eye sensations were the first to go, then the numbness in the temples. His remaining slight complaint was gas in the stomach.

This is a slight case of hypochondria produced by anxiety and guilt feelings relating to the hospitalization of a brother. This is one of the very few cases where there seems to be no link to the patient's childhood, although this is probably due to incomplete history-taking. One can speculate that the paranoiac-schizophrenic brother may have had symptoms of his illness during childhood and adolescence, which may have affected the patient in ways that rendered him vulnerable to hypochondria.

A forty-five-year-old house painter complained of tight feelings in his hands and spells of weakness. "Something dragging and pressing on my head. My eyes feel as though there was something in front of them. My throat comes up and chokes me. My voice changes and gets rough. I feel all worn out. One testicle is swollen up."

The patient had had many grievances in life. He wanted to be a lithographer, but was obliged to do manual labor. In addition to his wife and three children, he was supporting an alcoholic brother. He was in debt and his married life was unhappy. He said his wife was frigid and his children irritated him. He had had very little work during the past three months.

He was a quiet, resentful-looking man, and appeared anxious and worried. He improved after several interviews in which his difficulties were discussed, and he received emphatic assurance that "things were bound to get better."

This case has definite paranoiac features, but the hypochondria seems unrelated to them. It was the expression of his tensions and anxieties related to his unsatisfactory marriage, his lack of sufficient work, his worries about debt, and concern about his alcoholic brother. Again, there are no childhood data, but the alcoholism of the brother may be an indication of early problems.

A thirty-one-year-old man complained of "innumerable" pains, dating from his loss of sexual desire for a woman who wanted to marry him two years ago. "Dizzy head, like something buzzing; terrible headaches. It's the eyes and nerves alongside my eyes. It's taken my passion away from me. My face is changed, my hair is gray and weak. My teeth are just like enlarged stones; there is not enough room for them. I have tried to pull them out."

He didn't believe there was nothing physically wrong with him. He thought it was all due to meningitis. He had been to many hospitals and clinics in search of treatment, hitchhiking from Texas to Maryland. At other times he lived with his parents, did odd jobs, and kept snakes for a hobby.

He remembered nothing about his childhood before age sixteen. He never returned to the clinic and nothing could be done for him.

This is a diffuse hypochondria triggered by loss of potency, but it is more than likely that his loss of early memories is due to a severe neurotic, perhaps even psychotic, syndrome, to which the hypochondria may or may not be related.

The thirty-seven-year-old wife of a successful businessman had herself admitted to a hospital with the complaint, "My body is run down. I don't digest well. I can't sleep at all." She stated her complaints with much weeping, anxiety, and apparent depression. Six months earlier, she became deeply worried that her child might catch polio, and she began to lose weight. Two months later, she cut her finger, which was followed by a brief episode of cancer phobia. At the same time, she became intensely worried about her child's promotion at school. She became depressed and had symptoms of insomnia, constipation, and general bodily preoccupation.

After admission, she showed definite increase of depression in the mornings. Her topic of worries changed from day to day. For a few days, all her attention and complaints were focused on her slight hemorrhoids. When these were treated, her attention became concentrated on her menstrual period, which she considered to be not as ample as it should have been. This gave place to equally intense worry about homesickness.

There was a family history of depressions in her father and one brother. She was the youngest child, somewhat spoiled, and regarded as sickly by her mother, without any evident reason. She was always very concerned about her body. At age twenty-two, she developed an intense fear of TB. She had a delayed convalescence after having her only child at twenty-five. At thirty-five, she stayed in bed for a month to gain weight.

She improved steadily in the hospital on a regimen of reassurance and occupational therapy. Upon discharge, she was advised to increase her interests, but there was no follow-up.

This is a pure hypochondria, rooted in childhood, which did not become fixed in any system, and is complicated by depression, which is probably unrelated to it. It can be taken for granted that the hypochondria returned shortly after her discharge.

A fifty-year-old clothing designer was admitted to a hospital complaining of difficulty in swallowing, weakness, and rectal preoccupation. Physically, he had a healed rectal fistula, and no clinical signs. He objected to washing, was partially incontinent of feces, and constantly belched and passed wind. "My fistula is corrupting my privates, it has corrupted my whole being. I haven't the strength to swallow. I feel pretty weak around my heart. My blood is very poor. I always have a saliva taste in my mouth. Passing urine is not controlled."

He was the oldest of five siblings, two of whom have had depression in a setting of financial difficulties. He had gonorrhea at twenty and the operation for rectal fistula at forty. He married at twenty-six, but was sexually promiscuous until he became impotent, four years before admission to the hospital. He was an alcoholic for fifteen years, and became anxious, worried, and insomniac after a financial loss. This was followed by many bodily symptoms and many medical consultations. He became afraid of germs, very faddy about food, and diffusely hypochondriacal. Two years earlier, he became preoccupied with his rectum and dirty in his habits.

In the hospital, cleanliness and routine occupational therapy were enforced, and in addition he was given relaxation exercises and psychotherapy, all of which combined to control his incontinence. Still, upon discharge his mental state was essentially unchanged, and no real improvement has occurred since.

This patient's comment about the fistula corrupting his genitals indicates that his hypochondria is at least in part symbolic of his impotence. Although there is no information on his early life, the factors of promiscuity, alcoholism, and depression—also present in two siblings—signal a potentially troubled family constellation.

A forty-eight-year-old businessman was admitted to a hospital after he drank rubbing alcohol with suicidal intent. He reproached himself for the attempt and insisted that he ruined his eyes by it. On admission he said, "My melancholy is so deep that I feel hopeless." The ophthalmologist was able to reassure him to some extent, but he continued to complain about his eyes.

The patient had a long history of depressions; the suicide attempt was the culmination of his fourth. Each depression period lasted six to eight months and recurred about every two years. He had made one previous suicide attempt.

He was the fifth child in a family of six, and his mother's favorite. She impressed upon him at an early age the need to be ambitious, and he did extremely well at school and became class president. He was a salesman and did very well, eventually establishing his own business. He then formed the pattern of having a few very successful years in business which would be followed by a bout of depression, during which the business would be ruined. He repeated this cycle three times. An older brother had a depression lasting several months, another brother had two depressions, each lasting a few months. One sister had phases of extreme worry and agitation at her menses. Two other sisters were high-strung worriers. Two maternal aunts committed suicide during depressions, and the mother had always been tense and worrisome.

The eye complaint was his only hypochondriacal preoccupation; he said that the suicide attempt had injured a nerve in his throat, and this had affected his eyes, which, in turn, kept him from sleeping. His depression responded to drug therapy and counseling, but his hypochondria was intact on discharge.

Monosymptomatic hypochondria, that is, one with only a single complaint, is rare, but the eye has a special significance to some psychoanalysts. Greenacre emphasizes that the eye complaint is often an expression of guilt, frequently of a sexual kind. It may also have been a guilt reaction to his suicide attempt. Guilt is almost invariably characteristic of individuals who have been inculcated with the belief that they must be ambitious and successful and, in this case, that belief was also the probable source of his depressions.

Adult Hypochondria as Seen in Private Psychiatric Practice

A thirty-two-year-old contractor was referred to a psychiatrist by his family doctor when he developed fear of his neighbors and became restless and excitable. Two weeks before being seen, he became terrified when his dog barked and he thought his neighbors were trying to get at him. Three days later he took saltpeter, because he said he heard the neighbors tell him to, in order to prevent him from masturbating. After this, he couldn't sleep and spent the night prowling around the house, looking for trespassers.

In the opinion of the psychiatrist, the patient's orientations, memory, retention, and judgment were good. When asked what was the cause of the trouble, he said, "It might be self-abuse, but I might be just naturally nervous." He did not resist the suggestion that the trouble might have more to do with his "nervousness" than with the malevolence of the neighbors.

On his third visit, he admitted that he had been suffering from belching, nausea, "sharp shooting pains in the head as though someone was twisting it," off and on for several years. It was possible to reassure him, and treatment proceeded according to a diagnosis of paranoia: Every effort was made to gain and retain his confidence; he was emphatically reassured on immediate difficulties, such as masturbation, when he was told that it did not matter whether he did it or did not. The body complaints were utilized as something for which he needed help and care was taken not to argue with him, or deny his paranoiac delusions, but rather to inject doubt in them by suggesting that there were other ways of interpreting the facts. He definitely gained considerable relief from discussing his difficulties.

In the family history, the father was depicted as a morose, moody man, impotent for the last ten years, who got on badly with the mother. The latter devoted all her attention to the patient, her favorite among six children. The patient was a healthy child and showed no neurotic traits. He did not do well at school and dropped out at fifteen. From the age of twenty, he masturbated once a month with much guilt, and occasionally went to prostitutes. At twenty-seven, he got nervous and trembled for a few weeks following a case of gonorrhea, which was successfully treated. He had one love affair at twenty-two, but it was broken off, and he felt he did not want to marry.

He did well as a patient, gained insight, and he could discuss various factors in his life, such as sexual adjustment, his lack of relationships, and his incapacity for forming them, without agitation. His body complaints recurred from time to time, but he did not seem too bothered by them.

The body symptoms in hypochondria associated with paranoia are interesting in that they take on a typically paranoiac form of "as though." Also, they are diffuse and do not resemble any organic condition. They coincide with the flare-ups of paranoia. The paranoiac ideas are expressed first, followed by the body symptoms, followed by the description of the provoking incident. When this was fully discussed, the body symptoms would disappear in this patient, even before the conclusion of the session. This illustrates the importance of analyzing the hypochondria in paranoia, and viewing it as a condition that must be discussed and dealt with.

A thirty-year-old single accountant developed an alarmed concern over a rash that appeared on his legs after he participated in sex play, without intercourse, at a dance. He further developed bizarre hypochondriacal preoccupations, became dazed and anxious, and heard voices talking to him from great distances.

At this time, the only woman he had been interested in refused him. He developed pain in the back which spread to his abdomen and groins. He visited a doctor who used cystoscopy during the examination, which alarmed the patient greatly. He began to worry about his sexual capacity, and his work began to feel like a dream. He developed the idea that the two sides of his body were different, the right side strong, the left side weak.

His chief complaints were, "I haven't been feeling good. I have a pain in my back; my stomach has changed its shape. The fluid has gone out of my testicles into my rectum. The left side of my body is a woman, the right side a man, and my genitals are a little boy."

Family history showed that his mother died nine days after his birth, and he rarely ever saw his father, who was emotionally unstable. The father had disappeared on his wedding day and was found suffering from amnesia several months later. He was still living and remarried, but showed no interest in the patient. A maternal grandfather had a mental breakdown, was hospitalized, and recovered.

The patient was taken into the home of an uncle and aunt, who spoiled him. He had few playmates and developed a capacity to amuse himself by imaginative, solitary games. At fourteen, following the onset of masturbation and severe guilt reactions, he had a six-month period imagining his blood being turned into a snake. During his junior year in college, he suffered from peculiar sensations all over his body, which subsided in a few weeks. By the time he became an accountant, he had to take care of his paralyzed foster mother, who had become exacting and querulous. Five years later, he had influenza, transmitted it to his foster mother, and she died of it. The symptoms that led to his psychiatric referral had begun after the funeral.

It is interesting that this schizophrenic patient's hypochondria began at age fourteen as a result of masturbation guilt. The treating psychiatrists believed the guilt was rooted in the death of this patient's mother and the lifelong rejection by his father and the masturbation was merely a symbolic device for releasing guilt. Both the schizophrenia and the hypochondria came into full play when guilt flooded the patient, as it were, after his foster mother's death. There are so many pathological factors in this patient's childhood that the prognosis cannot be optimistic.

A fifty-five-year-old man was referred to a psychiatrist when he fell into a "depressive rut." For the past three years he has been under heavy strain, stemming from the responsibility of having to take care of his deceased brother's family. He complained of feeling tired out and appeared to be depressed. He believed he had a cancer and that he would not get well. He was becoming more and more agitated and was unable to work or sleep.

There were few childhood data, because this psychiatrist is existentially oriented and does not delve into the past. All we know is that the patient had a normal childhood, although he complained of a pain in his side from age thirteen to twenty-two, at which time he underwent an appendectomy. He suffered from constipation all his life, and showed considerable concern about his gastrointestinal tract. He has been drinking for thirty-five years, but never got drunk. He never married and was very apprehensive about his new responsibilities. His father was also an alcoholic and died at seventy-five. A paternal aunt spent one year in a hospital with a diagnosis of depression. The entire family suffered from hypertension.

This patient appears to have been hypochondriacal since age thirteen; he was always very particular about his diet and the care of his body. When his depression occurred, he interpreted his discomfort as body pain, which he considered to be cancer—a hypochondriacal notion consistent with the mood of depression.

The depression improved with treatment, but the fixed idea that he had cancer remained, although it did not interfere with his living a normal life. When he was asked how he was, he would always reply with a smile that he had cancer.

In this patient's long-established hypochondria, depression became a bodily pain, and the pain reentered the hypochondria in the form of a belief of having cancer. Once the delusion was formed, it outlived the depression. It illustrates once again that hypochondria can coexist with any number of mental and physical conditions, at times independently of them, at times interrelating with them.

A forty-one-year-old dancing teacher was referred to a psychiatrist during her fifth depression. Her first occurred at twenty-two, following an unhappy love affair, and the others took place in settings of financial and family difficulties. The fifth one occurred in the setting of having to look after an invalid aunt.

In the family history, one finds three very proud, independent, reserved, suspicious siblings, and similar personality traits in the patient and her father. She had always been concerned with her body condition, which was the chief reason for becoming a dancing teacher. Her depressions had been characterized by a paranoiac attitude. She felt that people had been doing things to irritate her and others were talking about her. Each depression lasted about a year.

The fifth illness showed symptoms of insomnia, constipation, inability to concentrate and make decisions, loss of weight, and extreme irritability. Her bodily complaints were: "My kidneys don't work right. Nothing about my body is good. I never have a natural bowel movement. I am worried about my stomach. The inside of my mouth and lips is raw. The doctors are not doing as much as they could for me." These complaints were stated aggressively, and she definitely had the attitude that it was the doctors' job to cure these symptoms, otherwise they were no good.

Her whole attitude was slightly paranoiac, in that patients in the waiting room were irritating her, everything was made difficult for her, and no one took the trouble of helping her.

The patient's depression was alleviated with drug therapy, but the hypochondria remained.

This hypochondria is interesting in that it is a depressive body complaint, but is also used as a form of self-assertion against doctors in particular, and the rest of the world in general, in accordance with the slightly paranoiac tendency of the patient's personality.

A thirty-eight-year-old wife of a physician was referred to a psychiatrist by her husband for treatment of her depression. She complained of "feeling blue," and of pains in her back. The family history showed one sister with numerous bodily complaints and a worrying disposition, and a maternal uncle with depression. She was the sixth child in a family of eight, did well at school, and developed an overconscientious, worrisome personality, very neat and orderly, reclusive, sensitive and reserved, and with few friends. She married at twenty, and had done nothing since, beyond looking after the home very efficiently and worrying about the children. Menses were irregular all her life and started at fourteen. Sexual intercourse was satisfactory until the birth of her last child, four years before psychiatric treatment. She had considerable difficulty and vomiting after that delivery, and she had been frigid since. At the same time, she began to complain of various bodily aches and pains, such as pain in her side, feeling weak, and occasional attacks of breathlessness and palpitations. She began to visit many doctors, even faith healers and all sorts of quacks, without any improvement. At one point, following a chiropractor's manipulations, she said she felt weak and sick, and that she was paralyzed. She stayed at home and acted like an invalid.

She became very depressed, tearful, irritable, and lost weight. She was constantly and unnecessarily worried about details and finances. At her first psychiatric session she expressed resentment against her sister, who she felt did not sympathize with her enough, and against her husband, who she felt bossed her around too much.

She complained of pain in the stomach and swollen eyes. "I have a lot of gas in my stomach; it chokes me. I worry about everything." She regarded her problems as being due to some physical illness, and said that she needed rest and quiet.

During several sessions, she gave an account of her sexual difficulties since the birth of her last child. She had been afraid of pregnancy, but refused to take contraceptive measures, and her husband had practiced coitus interruptus about four times a week without any satisfaction for her. Afterward, she would lie awake in an agitated and resentful state for the rest of the night. She had grown to resent her husband's domination of her and his not allowing her any outside interests. From time to time, she had dreams of catastrophes relating to her children and her husband, and sometimes of her throwing herself off a cliff.

After three months of therapy she began to complain of her piles, which were "real," and to focus all her bodily complaints on them. An operation was recommended and performed successfully. After the operation, she showed very great reluctance to recovery, and adopted a martyrlike attitude, craving sympathy from everyone. Her bodily complaints were not diminished, and the depression returned with suicidal ideas. After a period of improvement, during which she was given sexual counseling, she terminated therapy prematurely.

Here, the hypochondria seems to have developed in a setting of anxiety about sexual maladjustment and fear of pregnancy, together with the purposive factor of being able to manipulate and gain the sympathy of the husband. The effect of the operation was particularly interesting, in that the patient took the opportunity of relapsing into invalidism again, in spite of the psychiatrist's explicit emphasis on the need to divert her attention from her own body. Although childhood data are scant, her condition, coupled with her sister's high body awareness, indicates that the hypochondria may have been rooted much earlier than the record shows.

A twenty-four-year-old music student was sent to a psychiatrist by her parents who complained that she was overtalkative, overactive, and "indiscreet." Her father was a successful lawyer of aggressive personality and a past history of alcoholism. Her mother was very voluble, fussy, excitable, and hypochondriacal, and had spent a short time in a psychiatric facility. The parents quarreled constantly.

The patient was very close to her mother until the age of eight, when a sister was born. She had a violent jealousy reaction, hated her mother, and began to lie, steal, and have temper tantrums. She stole first from her sister's nurse, then from her mother, and finally from other girls at school. Nevertheless, she did well at school and displayed special musical talent.

She often stayed home from school for various aches and pains, mainly abdominal, over which her mother would make a great fuss. At fifteen, she simulated abdominal pain in order to avoid athletics at summer camp. It was taken to be appendicitis, and an appendectomy was performed. Ever since, she has been complaining of "dragging" pains in the abdomen and had frequent attacks of nausea, which would occur in any difficult situation.

She did well in music school, but was nauseous before examinations, even though she always passed them. One doctor ordered her to bed for one month for her abdominal complaints, another had her fitted with a special corset. A year before referral to the psychiatrist, her spirits began to rise. She gave numerous parties, talked constantly about herself, smoked and drank too much, and had several simultaneous affairs, including one with another woman.

During her sessions, she was excessively talkative, overactive, restless, aggressive, and boastful. She was facetious with frequent giggling. She was obviously extremely intelligent, and her mood showed very rapid changes, from elation to sadness and weeping, and frequent outbursts of anger. Bodily complaints were frequent; she was very body-sensitive and constantly watched her body sensations. These consisted of a feeling of her insides falling out, pain in the left shoulder, pain in the left breast, headaches, and intensely dramatized menstrual pains.

These complaints usually occurred in her depressed periods, and were always expressed dramatically and self-pityingly. It was generally easy to persuade her that there was no physical basis for them, and she would forget about them for a period of time. During six months of therapy, her moods evened out considerably, and the emotional instability improved. Treatment focused primarily on lessening her extreme attention to her body, and the hypochondria was markedly reduced.

This was an almost totally purposive hypochondria, a habit of complaint, which evolved out of the arrival of a sibling and was probably learned from the mother. It was not a symptom of her manic-depressive phases, which, in the opinion of her psychiatrist, were still another mode of expressing bodily complaint and coexisted with the physical hypochondria, serving the same purpose of attracting attention and love.

A thirty-eight-year-old married jeweler was referred to a new psychiatrist during his fourth mental illness. Family history showed a dominant mother, an excitable, worrying older sister, and schizophrenia in a cousin. He remained dependent on his mother all his life. He had no memories of his father, who died in the patient's infancy.

As a result of his strictly religious upbringing, he had great guilt feelings when he masturbated from the age of twelve. He was told by a teacher that syphilis, masturbation, and insanity were connected. At nineteen, he had a breakdown in college in a setting of anxiety about becoming a minister. He thought he was losing his mind from masturbation, but recovered after a few weeks. At twenty-one, when he started to work as a jeweler's assistant, he had a similar illness, and again at twenty-five, when he set up his own business and became intensely worried about his bowels.

His marriage has been uneventful. He was strictly religious, with a rigid moral code and he has always regarded himself as a weakling. Six months before referral he became depressed and developed a certainty of cancer. Three months later, this changed to certainty of syphilis. He had a series of bodily complaints during his first session: "I feel that I am going to die. I have no kidneys, my rectum is as tight as a drum. I used to have a cancerous growth, but it has been corrupted away by syphilis. Syphilis from masturbation, that's what it is." All this was told with a pleasant smile, which was totally inappropriate to the content of his talk.

The content remained essentially the same during four months of intensive psychotherapy and drug therapy. He was unable to gain insight or to recognize improvement. He was persistently urged not to reiterate his complaints, but to concentrate on performance and utilization of his assets, which were not inconsiderable. He withdrew from therapy prematurely.

This case of hypochondria coexists with flare-ups of schizophrenia which the patient has had since youth, and the content of which has remained unchanged. The hypochondria appears to be symbolic of the masturbation-syphilis-insanity axis that was established in his mind early, and chances are that it will neither get better, nor worse.

A twenty-one-year-old man of considerable means and no occupation was referred to a psychiatrist by his general practitioner when he began to complain that he had leukemia and that every organ in his body was diseased. He had numerous bodily complaints: "I am flabby; my legs are weak. I don't get any sleep and I lost my appetite. My teeth are rotten and full of holes; my left side is hollow. It's leukemia, isn't it? I am going down pretty fast." He was extremely fat and feminine in appearance. During the first interview, he was tearful, agitated, and depressed, saying that he would not get better and that he wanted to be buried next to his father.

At age fourteen, while he was in boarding school, his parents were killed in an automobile accident. An aunt became his guardian and he remained at the school, where he was often bullied because of his fatness and egotistical disposition. At fifteen, while at his aunt's home during a vacation, he caught a cold and thought it was the beginning of leukemia. He returned to school, however, and was sick with influenza for six days after arrival. After that, he complained of general malaise, and couldn't keep up with his studies. He ate very little, thought that the food was tampered with, and that others were talking about him. He was sent home, and on arrival followed his aunt around the house weeping, saying his teeth were full of holes, and that everyone was against him.

His father was a wealthy merchant and high-strung, irritable, and jealous. His mother was selfish and impulsive, unfaithful, and fond of good times. The young man had an early history of nail-biting and night terrors, but his younger sister was always healthy. He was originally sent to boarding school so he would be away during his parents' divorce proceedings which were aborted by the fatal accident.

He managed to graduate from boarding school, but did not continue his studies. He devoted himself fully to his hypochondria, going from doctor to doctor, in search of a cure for his leukemia. He had never thought of seeking psychiatric help, until he was referred.

After three years of treatment, the depression that was present at first lifted. He was able to discuss any subject without agitation, with the exception of sex, which he refused to talk about completely. The hypochondria did not improve, and all discussions took place within the framework of his assumed leukemia. He expects to die, but did not deny the possibility that a cure may be found.

This hypochondria was triggered by the parents' fatal accident and probably aggravated by his physical appearance and the bullying he received at school. There is a strong possibility that he has repressed some painful childhood memories relating to his mother's unfaithfulness, which may account for his totally negative attitude about sex.

Adult Hypochondria as Seen in General Medical (Nonpsychiatric) Practice

A twenty-year-old college student went to see a family practitioner, whose name he picked from the telephone book, and complained that he was afraid his heart would stop beating. He first noticed palpitations after being told a year and a half earlier that his stepfather might become permanently disabled, which would make him responsible for his mother's keep. At the same time, he lost a job that enabled him to attend college, and he had to drop out. He spent much time by himself, brooded over his frustrated college ambitions, and became very conscious of thumping and irregular heartbeat. He went to the library to look up the literature on irregularity of heartbeat, which frightened him.

Soon after that, while brooding in his room, he suddenly felt faint, his face burned, his heart thumped rapidly, he broke out in a sweat, and thought he was going to die. He called for his mother, who tried to comfort him. The attack lasted about half an hour, and when it began to recur with increasing frequency, he decided to go to a doctor for the first time.

His chief complaints were: "It's these loud heart thumps. I hear a thump and a gurgle, and I think my heart is going to stop. I feel my blood buzzing through my legs and I get jumpy feelings all over my body. Food gives me pain and forms gas. At night, food sticks in my right side. I have a kind of tired feeling; my legs go to sleep. I have white spots in front of my eyes." He was intensely agitated and worried by the symptoms.

No abnormality was found, but he was not relieved by the diagnosis of physical health on his second visit. Family history revealed no psychopathology. He was the only child of his sentimental and oversolicitous mother, who married his uncle on the death of his father when the boy was ten. He always did well at school and college before he had to drop out. He was always interested in his body. At fourteen, he began to watch his bowel movements closely, and exercised daily to keep fit. At sixteen, he complained of a funny taste in his mouth for several months, and thought there was something wrong with his stomach. As a direct result of reading ads and seeing commercials, he often worried whether his breath or body had an unpleasant smell. He had practiced masturbation since thirteen, but had no conflicts over it; nor did he have any particular interest in women.

He was told emphatically that he had no physical illness, that he had to ignore his symptoms and behave normally, and that his complaints would go away. His ambitions and difficulties were discussed, and it was suggested that they might be related to his symptoms. He seemed to cease worrying over his body in the course of subsequent visits, but he continued to anticipate trouble.

Despite the physician's optimistic prognosis, the vulnerability of this patient to hypochondria was established in early adolescence and is not very likely to go away. The death of his father and his mother's marriage to a brother-in-law had to be traumatic for a ten-year-old boy. And in addition the mother was oversolicitous. What the physican did seem to cure was anxiety attacks provoked by the possibility of the mother's becoming dependent on him, thus reversing reality. His basic hypochondria may not even have come into play during this crisis.

A twenty-two-year-old farmer's daughter, with complaints of choking sensations, was sent by her mother to the family doctor in a small town of twenty-five thousand. On examination she said she had these choking sensations whenever she was worried, and, in addition, she had a series of obsessive and compulsive symptoms, such as, a fear of being left alone lest she should swallow something harmful, a fear of swallowing pins and pills, and a compulsion to reread the last line of every page.

The first compulsive thought occurred when she kept thinking that she had not turned off the lights at school. This was in a setting of first going to high school, three months after her father's death, which had upset her greatly. She did very well in school, and was always worried if she did not head her class. She was of a worrying, overconscientious, overcautious personality, and was much fussed over by her mother. She developed other compulsive symptoms throughout high school, but they did not interfere with her life. It was not until she left home to attend teachers college, and took up work which was really beyond her intellectual abilities that she developed her constant choking sensations. She went home after a week and was unable to do anything but sit and brood. At this time, her mother sent her to the doctor.

In the doctor's opinion, the family history was negative, except that her mother, an ex-schoolteacher, was very excitable and excessively anxious about and ambitious for her daughter. She was the oldest and favorite child in a family of seven.

After a few visits, she was able to accept the suggestion that symptoms of choking and fear of swallowing were substitution devices she used, to avoid thinking about her real situation, especially the difficulties of becoming a teacher, and repressed sexual desires. She was reassured by a frank discussion of sexual problems, and her symptoms disappeared. When last seen, she was planning to take a business course.

It is uncommon for a hypochondriacal complaint, such as choking sensations, to occur with obsessional thinking, as the obsessions usually occupy the patient's attention completely. It is also difficult to agree with the physician's optimism in this case. The family history, which includes death of the father during the patient's early adolescence, an overanxious mother, and being the favorite child, of whom more is expected than she is able to deliver, contains enough psychopathology to doubt that a cure has been achieved.

A thirty-year-old man had been leading a totally inactive life for the past eight years, and for the past year had not left his house, owing to complaints for every part of his body. He was living off the earnings of his seventy-year-old father, who eventually forced him to see a doctor.

On examination, he was a healthy-looking, even athletic, man. His complaints were: "My shoulders and neck get drawn up, knotted, and helpless. My left foot is numb and sore. My calf gets drawn up and there seems to be no circulation. The trouble is on my left side, from the top of my head to the sole of my foot." The complaints were recited self-pityingly, and he appeared to want to hold on to them.

All that was known about his past history was that he had been very dependent on his mother, who died when he was ten. His personality was reserved, quiet, and obedient. Eight years ago he had attempted intercourse with a prostitute, but was terrified of venereal disease and was impotent. He was reassured that there was no need to be terrified of VD these days. And he was told to seek employment immediately. This was the only visit he paid to the doctor, and nothing further is known about him.

This is a hypochondria that symbolizes an intense fear of sexual activity and was triggered by the first sexual experience. His childhood dependency on his mother, substituted for by his financial dependency on his father, is a classic theme in hypochondria, and this patient certainly appears to be a chronic case.

The twenty-year-old daughter of a lawyer complained to her family physician of belching, stomach pains, and weakness. When approached, she breathed deeply, swallowed air, and belched noisily. Her expression and her attitude were pained and filled with self-pity. Physically, she was very tall, underweight, and had the hair and breast development of early puberty. Her complaints were: "My stomach hurts all the time; it's awful tight. I have sharp pains around my stomach, and they keep taking my breath away. I belch all the time." When questioned closely, she had complaints for every part of her body. When asked about her chest: "I have pains there"; her legs: "I have pains in the knee sometimes"; her head: "Just dizzy." When all tests proved negative and she was given the results, it made no impression on her. She said she was afraid she would not get better.

For the first eight years of her life, she was the youngest child and was spoiled and pampered by her self-sacrificing and over-solicitous mother. She was always regarded as somewhat of an invalid, after having had feeding difficulties as an infant. She was always constipated, and her mother gave her milk of magnesia several times a week. Both she and her parents were churchgoing Catholics and she had no definite information on sex. When she was seventeen, she was somewhat upset at a party when a man made advances to her older sister.

The latest series of complaints that brought her to the doctor began a week before the start of her junior year in college, when she complained of abdominal pain. She was put to bed and streptococcal infection of the kidneys was diagnosed. She remained in bed for two months, constantly complaining of pains to her mother, who waited on her hand and foot. By the time she decided to leave her bed, she was so far behind the curriculum that she skipped the fall term.

The doctor sensibly urged her to pay attention to what she was doing rather than to her bodily sensations, and to enter a regular routine of activities, including sports, studies, dating, but no fundamental change had occurred when she was seen a year later.

An unceasing desire for sympathy, a need to avoid school, and to be the center of attention are probably the main factors in this patient's hypochondria. However, her need for psychotherapy is clear, as one can trace her present belching complaints right back to her feeding difficulties in infancy. Symbolically, she appears to need to be burped constantly, and she lacks insight into her needs and motives.

A forty-year-old married woman was spoiled and pampered as the youngest child and only girl in her family. She developed a lifelong habit of bodily complaints as a means of attracting attention or avoiding difficulties. She would stay in bed several days with each menstrual period. After a number of sexual and romantic experiences, she married at thirty a good-natured but alcoholic rancher. Soon after the marriage, she simultaneously developed severe jealousy of her husband and frigidity. She complained even more about her body and visited many doctors for various aches and pains. A case of appendicitis and a slight injury in an accident combined to increase her invalidism.

Within a five-year period, she had her gallbladder removed, underwent hemorrhoidectomy, and lost the use of her legs and arms for a few months in a setting of jealousy, probably owing to hysteria. After that, she developed a case of paranoiac delirium, stayed in bed, and was often visited by her family doctor. The husband refused to allow hospitalization.

In a few weeks her delirium was over, but thinking difficulty, decision-making difficulty, and mental fatigue remained. At no time was a hypochondriacal complaint absent. Examples: "This nerve in my left leg is awful. I have a pain in my right shoulder. Supposing my gallbladder was cancerous? I feel there is a space between my brain and skull, and it's filled with tingling nerves." During her delirium, she interpreted her hypochondria on a paranoiac basis: "I thought they were burning me alive."

Treatment was directed at reducing her body concern and increasing physical activity, and she was also prudently counseled about her jealousy.

This case shows the evolvement of a loosely organized paranoiac delirium in a hypochondriacal personality, and the continuation of the hypochondria through the delirium. The hypochondria—a classic, pure case—also served the purpose of promoting chronic invalidism, a lifelong strategy for coping in this patient.

A thirty-four-year-old woman complained of pains in the chest, dizziness, and headache to a doctor who had not seen her before. She appeared to be an excitable, emotional person. "I feel really funny in my chest," she said. "I have headaches and feel dizzy. My eyes hurt, my head goes around like a wheel. Sometimes I have a cold feeling of dead hands touching my thighs."

As a child, she did not start talking till four and cried often. She did badly at school and suffered from headaches even then. She worked in various clothing stores, but often changed jobs, because she felt people were talking about her. She married at twenty-one, but did not get on well with her husband. Intercourse was distasteful to her and she developed abdominal pain. A year later, she had an appendectomy, and complained of numerous pains after that.

She bore two children, and her husband persuaded her to have two abortions, which was against her Catholic principles. He deserted her after three years of marriage, and she has been living with her parents since. On this particular visit, she was upset, because, she claimed, her husband was writing letters slandering her to her children.

She was seen on two more occasions by this physician, and treated with tranquilizers and verbal reassurance. On the last visit, the record showed no symptoms.

This is clearly a case of lifelong hypochondria, and this record of her kept by this particular doctor is likely to be only one of many. Her condition seems to be aggravated by paranoiac symptoms and severe anxieties related to sex and her abortions. No data have been recorded of her parents and family.

A fifty-six-year-old man complained of fits and headaches to a general practitioner who had not seen him before. The first attack had occurred eight years earlier when the patient started a restaurant business, after giving up a job as a mechanic because of lumbago. It consisted of a twelve-hour attack of unconsciousness, after which he returned to work at once, without medical consultation. Five years later, in a setting of financial difficulty, he became restless and irritable, and a doctor supposedly told him that he might have a stroke. A few months later, during the night, he had an attack of nosebleeding, which was followed by twelve hours of unconsciousness. Again, he returned to work immediately, without consulting a doctor. Six months later, when a store he owned was failing, he began to have attacks of sensations of pressure inside his head, after which he would lose consciousness for periods of ten minutes to four hours. These continued until he sold his store, then ceased, then started again when he started another store. Recurring attacks led him to give up that store, and at that point he visited the doctor in this account.

A complete examination, including EEG, was made with negative results. His wife, who supported him by her work, was very sympathetic toward him in his illness, though previously she had been in the habit of scolding him often.

He was a fat, anxious-looking man, and gave the impression of being dishonest and evasive. He complained of "terrible pain in the head that never leaves me. I thought there might be a cancer of the brain." His history revealed that his lumbago began at sixteen, and he attended many chiropractors for temporary relief. The lumbago vanished when the fits and headaches began. He first married at twenty, but deserted his wife and six children ten years later. He married a widow who, in his words, realized that "I must not be excited and would work her fingers off for me." There was a ten-year period of alcoholism during his first marriage.

The doctor diagnosed his condition as hysteria and treated him with hypnosis, which, according to the record, relieved both his headaches and fits.

It is extremely rare for hysteria to appear at age forty-eight, and then there is the matter of the lumbago that gave way to the fits and headaches to be accounted for. Lacking childhood history, one can only suspect the possible existence of the oft-encountered dependency link to the mother, inasmuch as dependency was to become the steady theme of his life. He deserted the only situation in his life where others were dependent on him, and his symptoms are closely connected to failed business ventures, which, had they succeeded, would have made him independent. This is clearly a case of early-onset hypochondria which acquired an additional dimension when it succeeded in gaining his wife's support and sympathy.

A twenty-eight-year-old woman had been having recurrent vaginal symptoms for five years, and eventually refused intercourse with her husband six months before visiting a gynecologist—the seventh she had seen since her condition appeared. She complained of pain, burning, itching, and general discomfort, and was given the entire spectrum of diagnostic tests—all with negative results.

Over the years, she had been treated with almost every drug used for vaginal infections and developed "allergic" reactions to them. The reactions included nausea, itching, burning, and swelling of the genitalia. But, neither physical examination nor culturing turned up any pathology.

History showed that the patient was an only child of a couple consisting of a severely hypochondriacal, almost invalid, mother, and a rigid father who was brought up in Central Europe according to Victorian principles of child-rearing. The mother was constantly preoccupied with her body, and the child witnessed many a self-administered vaginal douche throughout childhood and adolescence. She was always greatly embarrassed by this practice, and by the time she reached late adolescence, she developed a positive dislike for her mother. Her feelings toward her father had been largely repressed, as he was a cold, remote, unaffectionate person.

She married at twenty, while still in college, just to get away from home. However, her husband turned out to be a rigid, controlling type of person, who insisted that they have two children as soon as possible, after which he had a vasectomy. The patient's symptoms developed soon after the birth of her second child, and, even though she had been in psychotherapy since age nineteen, nothing helped her.

The gynecologist tried to guide her to the insight that her symptoms were an expression of her dissatisfaction with her marriage, but she resisted. He then referred her to a different psychotherapist, but there was no follow-up.

This is a case of second-generation hypochondria, where the child learns the mode and language of symptoms from a parent. This woman clearly wanted to get out of her marriage, she was "itching" to get out of it, but had not reached the stage where she was ready to recognize what her symptoms were telling her.

Closet Hypochondriacs

Closet hypochondriacs do not go to doctors and try to keep their condition secret. As a rule, they lead productive, often creative, lives. It is impossible to guess what the ratio of closet hypochondriacs to open hypochondriacs might be, but if the relative ease with which we found examples is an indication, then the guess is that the former may well outnumber the latter and definitely equal them.

Usually, the secret of the closet hypochondriac is known to, or shared with, one other person. Even when the person is unmarried, there is generally a confidant with whom, and only with whom, symptoms are freely and lengthily discussed. Some who are married attempt to keep the secret even from the spouse and believe that they have succeeded, whereas in fact they have not.

Spouses and confidants were the sources of these samples, and the cases have been sufficiently disguised to prevent recognition.

A forty-year-old single male closet hypochondriac has as his confidante his middle-aged secretary, who goes on long business trips with him. It is only during such trips that he opens up on the subject, usually after dinner.

She initiates the confessional with the simple question: "How have you been feeling?" and the answer may be as long as half an hour. "I feel I have something in the nature of a catarrh or colitis, which is giving me some sort of an infection. My circulation is all wrong because my extremities are always cold. If I do get a headache, I get a terrible headache and only fasting will help. A couple of weeks ago I was beginning to wonder whether my right kidney was affected. I had constipation and difficulty in getting a movement, and I had a terrible pain in the back." (This reminded him that he had gonorrhea at twenty-five.) "I got neuralgic pain in the testicles."

He was a premature baby, and at the age of two or three he was subject to bilious attacks and threadworms. He was not actually regarded as delicate, but he was not robust. At twenty-two he took over his father's substantial business, and soon after developed gastric disorders, physical weakness, and insomnia. One day, during the extraction of a tooth, he experienced a terrific "crack" at the right side of his head. While walking home from the dentist, he felt as if his shoes were too big for him. A few days later, he had an acute pain in the region of his gallbladder; the pain went right through to the back of his ribs and endured several days. He had "an awful attack of sickness" at that time, yet he never missed a day at work nor gave any outside indication of his condition.

For weeks at a time, he "lives on" castor oil, which is "like champagne" to him. He medicates himself extensively with non-prescription drugs, and has absolute confidence in them. Whatever his symptom may be, taking the self-chosen medication invariably relieves it for a time. On the road, he carries a special attaché case filled with his medications.

His father is seventy, and he speaks about him with admiration. The father's stomach "was always nervous and sensitive," but he is strong "as a bull." His mother, at sixty-five, is suffering from severe diabetes. A younger brother died; the oldest brother is strong "as a bull"; the third brother is "a wreck with his nerves and his stomach"; the fourth, fifth, and sixth siblings are all said to have "stomach trouble." His affections seem to be centered on his father and the younger brother who died.

His references to bowel function are especially frequent and striking. Besides those already noted, he mentioned what "magnificent stools" a certain food had produced for him. During a business trip to South America, he had "three big stools" a day "sliding through."

He likes women and has had several affairs, but, in his words, "could never bring himself to the point of marriage."

To all outside appearances, this is an energetic, fastidious, cheerful man, with a wide variety of interests.

This is a case of primary, early-onset hypochondria with diffuse symptoms, but strong emphasis is placed on anal erotic interests. His minute descriptions of stools are in striking contrast to his fastidiousness, a phenomenon known in psychoanalysis as "reaction formation." His single state, and his admiration for his powerful father and great attachment to his younger brother, may point to repressed homosexual tendencies, which may be a factor in keeping his hypochondria secret.

This thirty-two-year-old unmarried city employee lives with his mother and has never had any interest in women; nor has he had any homosexual experiences. His confidant is a member of his bowling team. They meet once a week, and after bowling have a few beers. His confidant is an open hypochondriac, and their weekly conversation is devoted almost exclusively to topics relating to the body.

He said that about ten years earlier he was about to sit down in a cross-legged fashion when he noticed a feeling "as if the muscles had turned around and were being pulled tight." He has never felt the same since. He said he had been constipated for a number of years and was in the habit of taking laxatives in large doses. He felt "upside down" while sitting on the toilet and claimed that he no longer had the desire to defecate, which worried him greatly. The lower part of his body "felt shortened altogether," and the "inner muscles" seemed to be drawn in.

He smiled often when relating bodily complaints, and used the term "as if" repeatedly. He seemed eager for reassurance, and whenever his confidant told him that he would be all right, he was visibly relieved. Meanwhile, he hadn't the slightest interest in his companion's complaints. Though he nodded frequently, it was obvious that he was not listening.

In annotating cases of closet hypochondria, we are hampered by knowing only what the confidant is told. In this particular case, we know nothing about childhood experiences and cannot even speculate on what might have caused the onset of hypochondria at age twenty-two. All we know is that this person lacked normal social and sexual interests and was content to live with his mother. His symptoms centered on the bowel, and, while his frequent use of "as if" may be indicative of paranoia, we have no information to confirm this. Meanwhile, he is a conscientious worker who seldom misses a day. He is good-looking and athletic, and, except for his confidant, no one has ever heard him complain about anything.

The case of this seventy-year-old retired lawyer is remarkable in that he had written his memoirs in his leisure time and then hired a free-lance writer to polish them, whereupon the writer discovered that the memoirs were almost entirely devoted to a hypochondriacal concern with the eyes and the head. When discreetly questioned by the writer, it turned out that the lawyer had been keeping a daily diary for the past forty-five years that listed and described in detail all complaints he had had, and yet he had never discussed them with anyone, nor mentioned the existence of the diary to anyone. He supplied this information quite casually, as if there were nothing unusual about it.

The lawyer is now dead, and his memoirs will never be published, hence it is possible to quote excerpts from them directly:

"July 8, 1939. My eyes continue to trouble me. Went to an

optometrist across the street, who has just opened shop. He said my
eyes are quite healthy and that I only needed a change of spectacles.
He gave me new ones, but they are no better than the old ones."
    "October 14, 1946. I visited N. today. Have not seen him in
fifteen years. Had a very lively talk. Felt no effect from it after-
wards, but had a very painful headache that night."
    "January 2, 1955. P. and his wife were staying with me for the
holidays; they just left. My head was bad every night while they
were here."
    "October 2, 1966. Lost all faith in optometrists. My eyes just
won't stop bothering me."
    This man apparently went from optometrist to optometrist
most of his adult life, yet never visited an ophthalmologist nor
complained to anyone. He never married, retired while still in his
fifties, and had a live-in female housekeeper.
    What little he had recorded in his memoirs about his family was
restricted to information about health. His father lived till seventy-
six, and was much given to attending to his own symptoms. His
mother also lived to the age of seventy-six, and suffered from
diabetes and rheumatism for a long time. One brother had died of
lung cancer. The entire family, he noted, was "rather given to
consulting doctors."
    Aside from the dominant theme of his eyes and headaches, he
had a pain in the right shoulder which persisted for many years, and
which he diagnosed as rheumatism. He never consulted a doctor
about this, or any other, complaint. For several years, he thought
that his heart was "defective," and refrained from all but the
mildest exertions.

It is difficult and perhaps unnecessary to comment on this
enigmatic case. It is clearly a lifelong primary hypochondria, and
the probability of childhood conflicts with the family is high.

    This forty-year-old housewife confided exclusively in her
daughter, who is her only child. Her husband of twenty years knows
nothing about her complaints.
    Her complaints are numerous and frequent: pain in the
stomach, pain in the back, difficulty in swallowing, throbbing in the
head, exhaustion on exertion, breathlessness, anorexia, hot and

cold flushes. Her father, who is still alive, is the kind of man who, in her words, "does not take much interest." Her mother, now dead, was domineering and occasionally cruel in the form of physical punishment.

She claims to have had convulsions and jaundice in infancy. Menstruation began at twelve and ceased at sixteen for three years. She went to work at fifteen and married at twenty. She was never interested in sex, and after she had her baby, she refused to have intercourse more than once a month.

Her daughter relates that throughout her school years she would find her mother in bed when she came home. She would call the girl to her bedside, hold her hand, and give vent to her complaints at length, always concluding them with a stern warning to keep these things secret from her husband. She would then get out of bed in time to prepare dinner, and acted like an energetic housewife when her husband came home.

She kept telling her daughter that doctors were a waste of money, yet whenever her husband had a physical complaint, she would invariably urge him to see a doctor.

Here, again, one can only speculate. She probably associated her father with her husband; the former "does not take much interest," and the latter cannot, because she does not tell him anything. The hypochondria probably originated with her health problems in infancy, and may have served the purpose of warding off her mother's cruelty.

This twenty-five-year-old single male salesman confided in his "best friend" only, even though he had two brothers within six years of his age, and a twin sister.

His chief complaint was "indigestion." He defined it as being always "full up," which was made worse by meals; feeling "rotten" was another frequent complaint. He often rubbed his chest to assuage the discomfort he felt there.

He never spoke about his family, and his best friend was never invited to his home. On one occasion, he referred to his maternal grandfather as "the laziest man who ever lived." Apparently, in the latter years of his life, the old man took to his bed altogether and got up only to relieve himself.

Despite his constant complaining to his friend, the salesman is a cheerful, energetic, and ambitious person who does well at his work, often earning bonuses. He has no interest in sex and pretty much keeps to himself. He claims he spends most of his time at home listening to records through earphones.

Although a lack of interest in sex seems to predominate among closet hypochondriacs, this should by no means be taken for granted. This sample is entirely random, and this particular characteristic should be regarded as coincidental.

A forty-two-year-old married restaurant owner reserves all his complaints for his wife, whom he married at thirty. Before that, he did not discuss his complaints with anyone. They have no children and plan none.

This man's complaints are so frequent and diffuse that it must be extremely difficult for him to save them up for the daily half-hour revelations upon going to bed. His aches keep moving from his head to every other part of his body. He feels his "insides are all wrong." He is certain that he has "uric acid" and "pleurisy on the kidneys." He has a very low self-esteem and feels ashamed for his symptoms, which is his reason for avoiding doctors or talking about them. He often says he is a "disgrace" and a "bad boy."

His father died many years ago and he has no memories of him, and he is exceedingly dependent on his mother to this very day. He often visits her, even though it involves uncomfortable and long travel. His relationships with his friends are also of a peculiarly dependent kind. He does very much as they want him to do and falls in line with their arrangements.

He is very much in love with his wife, and she with him. She does not mind listening to his complaints and comforting him gives her pleasure. He is knowledgeable and successful in his business. People come from long distances to eat at his restaurant and find him to be amiable, outgoing, and pleasant.

This is another classic hypochondria rooted in dependency to mother, a relationship he not only sustained but also transferred to his wife and friends. There is no evident explanation for the factor of shame, which keeps him in the closet, and one can only speculate about anality.

Conclusions from Case Histories

1. Hyponchondria can occur at any age in both sexes.

2. Hypochondria can occur either as a separate, independent disorder, or it can coexist with any number of mental and/or physical disorders. (No one will dispute the proposition that one can have manic-depressive illness and a head cold at the same time, yet, despite the evidence, resistance will be high to the claim that one can have hypochondria and a head cold at the same time.)

3. For hypochondria to occur, there is likely to have been:

    a. Exposure in early life to persistent complaints and/or actual evidence of illnesses within the family;

    b. Actual experience of frequent illnesses, including numerous contacts with doctors and hospitals;

    c. A pronounced dependency relationship with a parent or parent substitute.

4. The suffering of hypochondriacs is genuine. Their anguish can equal that of patients suffering from life-threatening illnesses, and, in many cases, they exert truly heroic efforts to conceal it from others.

5. The case material supports the accuracy of Gillespie's definition of hypochondria, "Hypochondria is a mental preoccupation with a real or suppositious physical or mental disorder; a discrepancy between the degree of preoccupation and the grounds for it so that the former is far in excess of what is justified; and an affective condition best characterized as interest with conviction and consequent concern, and with indifference to the opinion of the environment, including irresponsiveness to persuasion," and makes it clear that it is *not fear of illness*.

V. The Doctor and the Hypochondriacal Patient

For indeed who is not a fool, melancholy, mad?

—*Robert Burton*

The interest of the medical profession in hypochondria reached its peak during the Renaissance, especially in England, when the doctor served in the dual role of healer and moral guide to his melancholy patients, in the tradition of the Platonic dialogue *Phaedo,* where Socrates points out that the physician should teach his patients about medicine and the body. Theoretical interest remained keen until the end of the nineteenth century, and psychoanalysts had their say during the first half of the twentieth, yet it is a melancholy fact that the hypochondriacal patient received better care, and certainly more attention, from his doctor in Elizabethan England than he receives in today's Elizabethan England or, for that matter, anywhere in the world.

Doctors today are uninterested at best and hostile at worst when it comes to hypochondria. With a few notable exceptions, the majority of practitioners hide their ignorance and confusion behind a facade of indifference. They were not taught anything about hypochondria in medical school, and they cannot learn from the confusing literature. Their only opportunity lies in the scientific and persistent observation of hypochondriacal patients, and only the doctors who take this opportunity ever learn to provide comfort, if not cure.

Often the attitude is one of genteel scorn and humorous patronizing, as exemplified in a much-applauded lecture delivered to the British Medical Association's annual meeting in 1956 by an eminent British psychiatrist, Richard Asher. In his lecture, titled, "Illness as a Hobby," he arbitrarily and artificially divides hypochondriacs into three groups: "genuine students," "chronic hypochondriacs," and those suffering from what he calls "chronic autogenous disease."

The "genuine student" takes up illness watching in the same way he might have taken up bird watching, according to Asher. He develops an extensive knowledge of X rays, blood tests, and other clinical procedures, and keeps private charts of temperature. When the illness is going well, and when the patient is intelligent enough not to misinterpret technical matters, it is a "harmless enough hobby," but there are few people who can study themselves sufficiently objectively to avoid becoming hypochondriacal. (The most bothersome aspect of the characterization of the "genuine student" is Asher's manifest ignorance of the psychodynamics of hypochondria.)

The "chronic hypochondriac" group is subdivided into the "rich hypochondriac," the "poor hypochondriac," the "eccentric hypochondriac," and the "chronic convalescent"—a hopeless jumble of sociology and diagnostics. The rich hypochondriac—needless to say it is a "she"—supposedly takes a grand tour of the large cities of Europe, visiting consultants. She travels with an enormous collection of documents—opinions from other consultants, assorted X rays and laboratory reports, and lists of self-composed symptoms. These women discuss consultants with similarly afflicted friends in the manner of those recommending a fashionable tailor or a smart hairdresser. To the consultants in private practice, they are a "familiar, tedious, and lucrative burden."

The "poor hypochondriac" is an outpatient who, instead of going to the local pub for a beer and a chat, frequents hospitals for "a glass of medicine and a chat with other outpatients." Asher approvingly cites the existence of an unnamed outpatient department where patients do not see the doctor at all unless they ask for him.

The "eccentric hypochondriac" fervently believes in nature

cures, osteopaths, herbalists, and the like, and is more concerned with the treatment than with the symptoms. He proselytizes constantly, but his "odd ideas are harmless."

The "chronic convalescent" is one who has had a long-standing organic disease—in other words, a "real" illness—which has become so familiar to him as to be "almost a friend." If the illness is cured, he feels suddenly deserted and friendless, and does not want to get well.

Asher's most pathetic excesses come to the fore in his self-labeled group of "chronic autogenous disease," which includes anorexia nervosa, chronic artifactualists, and Munchausen's syndrome. He talks of anorexia nervosa as if it were a joke, and uses a children's rhyme to illustrate his views:

> Not any soup for me I say
> O take the nasty soup away
> I won't have any soup today.

As for chronic artifactualists, they are people who deliberately anoint their skins with corrosive substances in order to create dermatitis, or burn themselves with caustics, or engage in other acts of minor self-mutilation—all of them clearly psychotic, not to be dealt with lightly as they are here by Asher.

Munchausen's syndrome is a subject of great hilarity for this eminent psychiatrist. It is, in fact, the strangest and rarest form of "chronic autogenous disease," named after (and subsequently misspelled) an eighteenth-century cavalry officer, Baron von Münchhausen, who was famous for his tall tales. Although some writers erroneously associate it with hypochondria, it is actually a psychotic disorder whose chief unconscious purpose is self-mutilation. The patient with this syndrome travels widely and tells dramatic and untrue stories to gain admission to hospitals. Most often, he is brought to the hospital by the police, having collapsed in the street or on a bus, with an apparently acute illness supported by a plausible and dramatic history. At first, his illness seems to be most convincing, but later it will be found to be false, and his symptoms and signs discovered to be entirely spurious. It will be found that he has attended and deceived an astounding number of hospitals. At several of them he was operated on, as witnessed by a collection of abdominal scars. So skillfully does he imitate acute illness, that quite often he is discovered only when a passing doctor or nurse recognizes him, having seen him at another hospital. At other times, doctors get suspicious because the patient is truculent or evasive, or because the symptoms are a little unconvincing. If he remains undiscovered, he will discharge himself within a few days and go on to the next hospital, using a different name, but telling the same false story, faking the same fictitious symptoms, and submitting to numerous examinations and operations.

Asher humorously coins separate labels for his three subgroups of Munchausen patients: The acute abdominal type who strive for exploratory operations (*"laparotomaphilia migrans"*), the type who specialize in internal bleeding (*"haemorrhagia histrionica"*), and those who simulate neurological diseases (*"neurologia diabolica"*). "Maybe it is really a form of chronic tantrum like that of the angry child who bangs his head against the wall to show his resentment after something has gone wrong," concludes this scholar of illness to a round of hearty applause by members of the British Medical Association. This was the body which thirty years earlier sponsored a historic symposium on hypochondria.

If seemingly excessive space has been allotted to this pitiful public performance by a well-known psychiatrist, it was to dramatize the negative attitudes about hypochondria held by a great majority of doctors. Few of them are as technically ignorant on the subject as Asher, but their attitudes can be similar.

In the spring of 1977, a leading U.S. medical journal interviewed a number of psychiatrists on the subject of hypochondria and the results manage to summarize the state of knowledge and attitudes of American psychiatrists today. The chairman of a psychiatry department from the Southwest told the interviewer that the hard-core hypochondriac is someone who needs to be sick, who needs physical symptoms that allow him—or, *"more frequently, her"*—to depend on a doctor. "They keep coming back to the doctor and *kind of drive him up the wall with the ever-changing, unremitting problems.* He can never reassure them for any length of time, can never 'cure' them. They love to talk about themselves, their organs; they think other people are fascinated by their pains, their bowel movements, their blood pressure." (Italics mine.)

This psychiatrist understands the basic problems of hypochondria and addresses himself to them knowledgeably in the interview, yet his attitude is so negative and scornful that it is hard to imagine him actually helping a hypochondriacal patient. He makes a number of points prudently and cogently, and then remarks that hypochondriacs present an even more difficult problem to young doctors. Why? he is asked. Because, "although some doctors will *gracefully accept this burden,* the vast majority wait until a new man comes to town *to fob this group off on him.* One of the crosses young doctors have to bear is inheriting this collection of hard-core hypochondriacs the minute they hang up their shingles." (Italics mine.)

Doctors do not generally discuss this subject among themselves. The reason is that they feel so angry with these patients and at the same time feel guilty about being angry with people who cannot or will not get well. What happens all too frequently is that as the doctor gets more and more frustrated, he overmedicates the patient, does too many diagnostic procedures, and may even do surgery as a last-ditch attempt to placate the patient. The remark, "Let's take a look in there," has prefaced many needless laparotomies.

Another psychiatrist notes cryptically that the complaints of the hypochondriacal patient are "almost always subjective"—as if it were possible to complain objectively—and cites derisively the patient who had a low-grade fever that could not be traced to any organic cause: "Doctor, if they could only find something to explain this." When asked what he had in mind, the patient answered, "Well, like TB or some kind of rare infection. I'd even settle for a touch of lung cancer."

A California psychiatrist observes that many doctors swear that the diagnosis of hypochondria sort of confers immortality on these people—that they never die, that they never get cancer or strokes. Of course, this is not true, notes the psychiatrist, but they "usually do go on and on, or maybe it's just because they're such a bother to the doctor that he thinks they go on and on."

An internist at a famous clinic says a little prayer before examining the laboratory findings and X rays of hypochondriacal patients: "Dear God, please let this patient have gallstones." He wants to see X-ray evidence of gallstones or something so that he call tell these patients that there is a specific problem and specific surgery to correct it. "But, of course, these patients never have gallstones and this prayer is never answered."

Doctors are warned in the same interview to be prepared to see their hypochondriacal patients for years and years, to "grow old with them." One psychiatrist quotes his father, an internist, saying to such a patient, whom he had been seeing for some twenty years, "You know, you've had this doctor and that doctor, this one, that one. Do you know what they have in common?" She says, "No, what?" "They're all dead, and your complaints helped them along."

A psychiatrist interviewed during the preparation of this book always assumes that the chronic hypochondriac is masochistic. He feels the masochist's strength is in his illness, his ability to control others with his symptoms, his pride of self-sacrifice and hard work. No masochistic patient is readily going to give up his strength for the weakness offered him through cure.

According to this psychiatrist, the doctor must somehow convey to these patients that he is more interested in maintaining the relationship than in curing symptoms. To become concerned with the symptoms, whether they get better or worse, is to perpetuate these patients' belief that the flow of affection is directly linked to symptoms. They must not be promised cures or even improvement. Such an outcome is feared by these patients, because it is equated with discharge from treatment and, therefore, withdrawal of love. To avoid this problem, it may be best to allow them to decide for themselves whether they will come back or not, and how often, if they do.

These patients "doctor" themselves, prescribe and administer medications to themselves as an expression of self-concern and self-mothering. In a sense, they take care of themselves, for no one else is trustworthy, although they never cease to look for such a person. This psychiatrist believes that chronic hypochondriacs respond poorly to medication of all kinds; moreover, as a group, they have the highest incidence of drug-related side effects—a statement that cannot be supported by data. He recommends that drugs be used only when the patient shows signs of ego depletion, and then special care must be exercised in the use of the drug. Most of these patients already know what helps or does not help them and usually they have discovered it themselves. It helps to ask them about their preferences, because "it leaves them in control of the situation."

If drugs are given, the advice continues, they are invariably better tolerated when prescribed on a pessimistic, rather than optimistic, note. "I am not sure this drug will be of any use to you," the doctor should say to the patient, "but you can try it if you like." This is presumably far more effective than, "This medicine will help you," because the giving of a prescription is usually nothing more to these patients than testimony to their impression that the doctor simply wants to get them out of the office. It is more a rejection than a gift.

Furthermore, since the masochistic patient is much more ready to make a personal sacrifice than do something for his own good, medication is more likely to be taken if the doctor says, "This may help you regain enough strength to take better care of your children," rather than, "This will make you feel better."

This psychiatrist believes that the offer of another appointment is far more effective than drugs in the management of hypochondriacal patients. When appointments are given, whether or not symptoms are better or worse, complaints tend to diminish and there is evidence of improved functioning.

Still another chairman of a department of psychiatry at an important Southern university states unequivocally, and in the face of overwhelming evidence to the contrary, that the chief complaint of the hypochondriacal patient is likely to be a disease rather than symptoms. When "she" presents a symptom or is asked about it, she most often describes it in "medical or anatomical" terms picked up from the literature, rather than in ordinary sensory or physical terms. A backache, for example, is likely to be described as "rheumatic" or "sacroiliac," or a chest pain as "substernal" or "anginal." When pressed for more specific description, "the woman" tends to become impatient with the doctor for not identifying her problem. Whatever she may say, claims this psychiatrist, she means, "Doctor, I have a bad disease. Please diagnose and treat it."

When this patient is told that nothing is wrong, she will feel let down and disappointed, but she will not take no for an answer. She will either intensify her old complaints or acquire new ones, and if this fails to bring results, she will change doctors until she finds one who can make a positive diagnosis. When such a diagnosis is made and treatment is prescribed, the patient feels good, sometimes even elated.

The type of diagnosis and treatment desired by hypochondriacal patients varies according to the nature of the hypochondria, and this particular psychiatrist divides these patients into two categories: "ambitious hypochondriacs" or "sick hypochondriacs"—demonstrating once again that psychiatrists have failed to do their homework on hypochondria.

In this view, the goal of medical diagnosis and treatment for the ambitious hypochondriac is a definitive cure. The patient is not satisfied with an equivocal or tentative diagnosis, and does not cooperate for long with treatment of symptoms or nonspecific treatment. If medication is prescribed, she is likely not to comply, because she has a special predilection for surgery. When surgery is prescribed, she looks forward to it with great anticipation and pleasure, not because of a masochistic need to suffer, but because she thinks that, at long last, her problem is about to be resolved. After recovery, the elation wears off gradually with the realization that nothing has really changed, and she finds new symptoms, dissatisfied as ever. But the patient does not give up, and resumes her quest for a cure. And if she fails too often or too long, "she may even develop an overt psychiatric illness, such as depression or paranoia!"

The sick-role type of hypochondriac has less ambitious goals, according to this formulation. This patient seeks medical diagnosis and treatment primarily to sanction a sick role. In contrast to the more ambitious hypochondriac, the sick-role type is satisfied with a chronic disease and long-term symptomatic treatment. She has a special predilection for oral medication—the greater the variety, the better—and in time she will need other drugs to treat the side effects of the former ones. She cannot relax and just be sick; she constantly has to act out the sick role, and the best props she has for dramatization are her doctor, her diagnosis, and her medicine.

And what are the psychodynamics of this striking theory? The hypochondriac is simply "unhappy." Repeated frustrations of life have beset her. She has become thwarted either in her need for love and acceptance and for tangible possessions and advantages, or by her failure to defend herself against the aggression of others. The hypochondriacal solution is most likely to develop in individuals who tend to attribute all their frustrations in life to feelings of worthlessness. Consequently, physicians are advised to interpret the hypochondriacal symptoms as a symbolic representation of the patient's feelings of worthlessness. The mechanism of symptom formation is the "simple" displacement from the psyche to the soma of the feeling that there is something wrong with her as a person.

In another interview, another psychiatrist admitted that few doctors "like" hypochondriacal patients. They refer to them contemptuously as "crocks" and consider them the bane of medical practice, thorns in their flesh, to be mollified or passed on to some zealous newcomer as quickly as possible. These patients are regarded as overdemanding, irritably persistent, and ungrateful of the doctor's efforts. They often show a hysterical indifference to the symptoms, while remaining highly vocal concerning them. Paradoxically, in this view, anxiety in these patients is often not relieved by physiological or psychological explanations, but aroused. Indeed, a strong aversion may be displayed to explanations, and they appear to be angered by the doctor's attempts to assuage their fright or concern. They often manifest a negative reaction to medication, and seem prideful and happy, rather than frightened, that they have foiled the best efforts of doctors. They seem, sometimes, to take a "perverse pleasure" in this.

It is of interest that many of Freud's patients in the early days of his psychoanalytic practice had severe hypochondriacal symptoms and conversion reactions, the very problems that today's physicians have so much difficulty treating, and the very patients toward whom they display negative attitudes, strikingly similar to Freud's, who wrote:

> There are certain people who behave in a quite peculiar fashion. . . . When one speaks hopefully to them or expresses satisfaction with the progress of treatment, they show signs of discontent and their condition invariably becomes worse. One begins by regarding this as defiance and as an attempt to prove their superiority to the physician, but later one comes to take a deeper and juster view. One becomes convinced not only that such people cannot endure any praise or appreciation, but that they react inversely to the progress of treatment. Every partial solution that ought to result, and in other people does result, in an improvement or a temporary suspension of symptoms produces in them an exacerbation of their illness; they get worse instead of getting better. They exhibit what is known as a 'negative therapeutic reaction.'

Thus, it may not be frivolous to suggest that the present negative therapeutic reaction of medical practitioners to hypochondriacs stems from the past negative therapeutic reaction of hypochondriacs to their predecessors.

It is not surprising, then, that when a New England psychiatrist reviewed the patient records of an outpatient clinic attached to a large metropolitan hospital, he found a startling communications gap between hypochondriacal patients and doctors. One doctor noted on the record of a patient who had been coming to the clinic for years: "Patient comes here to waste some of our good time." Conversely, a patient who had had 829 appointments at 26 clinics in 33 years, appeared one day with the complaint, "I have a little trouble. . . ." Patients appear to be trying to satisfy a poorly defined need, and doctors are responding in ways that may be considered as sound medical practice but which are clearly not bringing about improvement. When it comes to hypochondria, doctor and patient seem to be working at cross-purposes, with the patient desperately looking for something, and the doctor almost equally desperately trying to get rid of people he does not regard as truly ill and whom he cannot help.

Even so, the medical profession has never held itself aloof from the investigation of the unknown because the subject matter evoked irritation and repugnance. Why, then, does it not confront the questions of why hypochondria evokes such uniform antipathy from doctors, and why, indeed, has hypochondria been so uniformly neglected? Much can be learned by examining the expectations of doctors and patients.

Patients go to doctors for many reasons. A visit is always characterized by some need or problem for which assistance is desired, but these needs and problems vary considerably. There is no single definition of the doctor's role, and there is a wide range of situations that people perceive as appropriate reasons for seeking medical attention. Individuals cope with their problems and difficulties in many ways, and seeking medical assistance is only one of many possibilities for dealing with distress. For example, in the case of closet hypochondriacs, medical assistance is *not* one of these possibilities. Whether a person views the doctor as a relevant helper depends on such varied factors as his cultural background, his personal characteristics, how he perceives and defines particular indications of illness, and the social and physical accessibility of the doctor, the personal and economic costs of seeking medical help as compared with alternative approaches to the problem, and many other factors.

The doctor's views are largely molded by his professional

training and clinical experience, but when the person with a problem becomes a patient, his views are influenced by the need to cope with that problem. Consequently, lay and professional attitudes meet, and sometimes clash, within the framework of the doctor-patient relationship. The definition of a given illness held by a physician sometimes differs from that held by a patient. The definition of an illness thus may take place in a context where there are competing views of the patient's condition, and the final resolution of the patient's problem may depend on how these different definitions come to be applied in a specific instance. This is not to imply that the doctor is unable to maintain his professional opinion in the situation, but that it will mean nothing if the patient does not respond to the doctor's expectations and does not cooperate in treatment.

We should also note that doctors also vary widely in their responses. They differ in their views of medicine and its relevance to a variety of problems, in their medical knowledge, in their understanding of particular subareas of illness, and in their training, experience, and philosophical perspectives. Moreover, medical knowledge itself is a mixture of scientifically precise facts and clinical impressions, leaving much room for medical uncertainty and individual variations to manifest themselves. How the individual doctor deals with such situations of uncertainty and ambiguity is contingent on his views and his personal and social characteristics.

Different personal and social standards for defining illness will influence *which illnesses are recognized,* who seeks care, and who seeks delay, in treatment for serious conditions. Whether it is the patient defining his own problem, as is often the case with hypochondriacal patients, or the doctor evaluating the patient's complaint, both attempt in one way or another to compare the problem with some standard of normality. In general, patients' evaluations of normality are based on their own experience and some synthesis of medical information. In contrast, medical norms are based on the results of clinical observation, field studies, and experimental investigation. Furthermore, the appli-

cation of medical norms to particular patients is further complicated by divergences in the physiological and psychological functioning of patients, who vary in age, sex, and way of life. All these
factors suggest that the concepts of normality and deviation from
normality are implicit in both lay and medical evaluations of
illness.

Most of the time, clear physical complaints and difficulties in
functioning are viewed as illness, and society in general rarely
holds people responsible or accountable for their physical ills.
Although from time to time individuals may not take necessary
precautions to avoid risks of illness, it is generally assumed that
illness is an event that happens to people and that it is not
consciously motivated. There are, however, conditions, such as
hypochondria, that raise doubts as to the appropriate perspectives to be used in evaluating a patient's complaint. In cases
where the patient complains frequently, but where it is difficult to
account for the complaint, questions will be raised in the doctor's
mind concerning the patient's possible desire to avoid obligations
and use illness as an excuse. He will, then, come to regard the
patient as a "malingerer" or a "crock," and his condition will no
longer be seen as an *event,* but as a motivated reaction.

The physician is supposed to treat illness without judging.
There is, however, an irreducible moral judgment in the designation of illness as such; the character of this judgment is frequently
overlooked because of the virtually universal consensus on the
undesirability of much of what is labeled illness. Cancer is so
obviously undesirable to everyone that its status as an illness
seems objective and self-evident rather than what it is—a social
valuation on which most people happen to agree. Even recogniz-
ing this, however, it must be observed that the word "illness" is
often used explicitly for the purpose of avoiding moral condemnation; by labeling alcoholism an illness and declaring the derelict
to be sick, the intention is to avoid moral condemnation.

Hypochondriacs and other patients who have a high inclina-
tion to use medical care pose a special source of difficulty for the
doctor. At some point, he will have to come to the conclusion that
the patient does not suffer from a tangible illness and decides not

to search for a physical cause any longer. There is no end to the number of diagnostic procedures that can be performed, and the doctor knows that while he can never really prove that there is no underlying physical basis, the probability of there being one is negligible. There is also the factor of the risks of continued exploration: dangers inherent in various diagnostic procedures, the economic costs, and the probability that continued searching may reinforce the attitude of the patient that he is, indeed, physically ill.

Many physicians feel profoundly frustrated in these circumstances, because they lack strategies for dealing with a patient who is not clearly ill. Thus, the relationship is frequently terminated with no attempt to seek the origin of the patient's trouble on a nonphysical basis, and the patient is informed that there is nothing wrong with him. While this may get the patient off the doctor's back, he will probably, and in most cases, he must, move on to another doctor, initiating the entire process once again, with its various associated risks. Since so many patients, and not all of them hypochondriacs, conform to this general portrait, developing more adequate strategies for dealing with them is one of the greatest challenges medicine faces today. In the complex equation created in illness by the needs of the person, his body, and society, physicians play a vital role. Having been assigned custody of the body, they are the ones who can make body demands legitimate. Physicians are the arbiters between the person and his body, and, as has been made clear by sociologists of medicine, they are also representatives of society and its values.

When the patient initiates the process of going to see the doctor, he contributes at least three important factors: (1) his objective clinical disorder and symptoms, as well as his perception, knowledge, beliefs, and attitudes about having a particular disorder or symptoms; (2) his attitudes and expectations of the doctor and medical services; (3) his definitions of health, illness, and the appropriateness of seeking medical help at that particular time.

The presence of an objective clinical disorder in itself is not a decisive factor. Community surveys have repeatedly noted large numbers of individuals, both aware and unaware of their disorders, who were not under medical care. A postwar study of a London district, which was preselected as healthy by census data, found that 91 percent of the population had a physical disorder when interviewed and medically examined. A more recent report of medical examinations carried out in ten thousand apparently healthy subjects showed that 92 percent had disease or clinical disorder that was amenable to diagnosis and treatment. Studies of selected industrial populations have similarly shown high degrees of prevalence. It may well be the fact that illness, judged by the prevalence of symptoms and signs, is the rule rather than the exception in "healthy" populations; and if that is the case, then, the individual's response to symptoms by seeking aid may be a more objective or operational definition of illness than our usual emphasis on the presence of symptoms and signs. Also, this gives rise to the question: In what ways is this individual different from the hypochondriacal patient?

Clearly, an objective clinical disorder is not a sufficient reason to go to a doctor. For many patients with bronchitis and emphysema, the "cigarette cough" is a norm and not a reason to consult a doctor. Such patients go only in advanced stages, when the symptom interferes with the performance of their usual tasks. Quite often, the basis for seeking medical care may be due more to a specific impairment of an equally specific social role, such as breadwinner, rather than concern with any underlying medical problem.

There have been many studies about what people expect of a doctor, and what qualities go into the designation of "a good doctor," but the results are scattered. There are so many sociocultural considerations that these questions cannot be answered at all in general terms. Most importantly, patients' expectations of doctors are seldom in line with the doctors' own conception of their role, and this disparity can and does lead to instances of mutual distrust which results in reluctance to continue treatment at that time or to seek advice in the future.

There is equally scant general knowledge about the particular set of circumstances that determine *when* the patient goes to the doctor, although there are many specific studies. To a large extent, it is evident, that ethnicity and social class are the decisive factors. For example, Italians tend to seek medical help when their symptoms interfere with social and personal relationships, or when they are experiencing a situational or interpersonal crisis. The Irish tend to go only after they have received the approval of others and the visit is sanctioned; Anglo-Saxons go primarily when they perceive an interference with some specific vocational or physical activity. Also, higher income individuals go to the doctor much more readily after a symptom appears than do lower income persons. In some cases, the decision revolves around a choice among shaman, minister, herbalist, chiropractor, homeopath, pharmacist, osteopath, or physician. In others, it is the choice between types of medical service, between public or private care, general practitioner or specialist, clinic group or private practice.

All these matters are relevant to the hypochondriac-doctor relationship, which is rarely studied. They are also relevant, because they point to the large gray area that surrounds definitions and perceptions of health and illness.

In what ways is the hypochondriac-doctor relationship significantly different from the relationship between a clinically ill patient and the doctor? At first, the hypochondriac demands attention, examination, diagnosis, and treatment for his complaint. When these are not forthcoming to his satisfaction—as, of course, they cannot be—the patient's mood is transformed from apparent hope to disbelief, distrust, and deception, from apparent respect to criticism and rejection, from a craving for reassurance and explanation that fit in with his own prognosis to the immediate resumption of his own method of treatment. This transformation is often so rapid that the two sets of attitudes almost blend together, as expressed by de Mandeville in the eighteenth century: "I have sent for you, doctor, to consult you about a distemper of which I am well assured I shall never be cured."

The doctor is not a trusted healer to the hypochondriac but a trained yet fallible expert. As the doctor addresses his expert ability to the case, he will soon be disqualified by the hypochondriac—an ambivalence that characterizes the hypochondriacal symptom formation itself. The doctor, in turn, can experience the hypochondriac as neurotic, psychotic, or even as psychopathic, observe him with disdain, doubt, or anxiety, and conclude that he is dealing with a case of delusion. Not having been taught about hypochondria in medical school and confused by the literature, he develops the negative attitudes discussed earlier.

Charles W. Wahl, who admits that doctors are unprepared to deal with hypochondriacs, offers the following mode of "coping":

1. The doctor should listen to the patient. He should encourage him to express his feelings with his mouth, rather than with his body. A willingness to listen is exactly what the patient wants and needs. As soon as he is reassured that the doctor is capable of attentive listening, his need for unreasonable amounts of time will greatly diminish.
2. Hypochondriacal patients, more than any others, need a continuous and dependable relationship of trust and confidence with their doctor. The doctor literally stands *in loco parentis,* and only he can repair the damage these patients have suffered in their parental relationships.
3. The doctor should listen carefully to what the patient says, especially to his idiosyncratic terms and expressions. These provide clues to the illness; the persons or situations he describes may alert the doctor to what fears or wishes the symptoms may symbolize.
4. The doctor should not equivocate about his diagnosis or suggest alternate possibilities. This will frighten the patient, and he will seek out another doctor.
5. The doctor should not overstudy the patient. Long and unnecessary workups will cause the patient to get worse. Such

procedures as spinal taps, bronchoscopies, cystoscopies, and so forth should be avoided. Patients feel assaulted by these procedures and are likely to develop hysterical complications.

6. Simple anatomical and physiological explanations, such as how a muscle spasm can produce the symptoms that concern them, can be vastly helpful. The doctor should never say that the symptoms and pains are imaginary, but rather explain how tension can produce pain and dysfunction.

7. The patients should be encouraged to examine their deepest feelings of fears and needs. They should be encouraged to verbalize them, along with other problems and difficulties. This may help them to see that focusing on health problems is a means of avoiding other areas of concern.

8. Medication should be used sparingly, if at all. These patients may be already dosing themselves with drugs obtained during doctor shopping.

9. If the patient has to be referred to a psychotherapist or psychiatrist, the doctor should learn how to make such referrals without threatening or humiliating the patient, and without seeming to abandon him.

No doubt, this is sound advice, although it contains nothing one cannot find in the medical literature of the Renaissance. Furthermore, it is difficult to see how such a time-consuming regimen could be applied within the framework of today's medical practice. With the exception of psychiatrists and psychotherapists, the conditions of a physician's practice do not allow enough time with hypochondriacal patients to make Wahl's advice practicable.

E. James McCranie believes that dealing with hypochondriacal patients involves a compassionate understanding on the physician's part that helps the patient gain insight into the meaning of his symptoms. He must be led to see their significance to him in dealing with low self-esteem and coping difficulties. A great deal of warmth and patience is needed, which, again, means

time. The patient cannot be expected to relinquish the hypochondriacal pursuit of a cure until the physician has helped him realize
that his frustrations are not due to his defects as a human being,
and that there are better ways of dealing with his problems. Nor
can the patient be expected to relinquish the use of illness as a
coping device until he learns more adaptive ways of coping with
his needs.

The recognition that hypochondria is a *serious* and *valiant*
attempt to resolve a real problem should help the physician to
avoid dismissing the patient as a crock who is imagining all his
difficulties. Nevertheless, there will be patients who cannot give
up their fixation on a hypochondriacal solution. In such cases,
understanding the hypochondriacal endeavor should help the
physician to maintain the patient on a neurotic level of functioning that is relatively safe and comfortable. This would require
acceptance and toleration of the patient's neurotic mode of
adaptation, the avoidance of overtreatment and undertreatment,
and attempts to help the patient keep his use of the sick role as a
coping mechanism within reasonable bounds. A stable
hypochondriac is better off than one who is miserable, hostile,
and demanding, or constantly in search of a new and more
understanding doctor. Parenthetically, it is of interest that the
Hippocratic oath says nothing of the doctor's responsibility to
cure illness, or to alleviate pain and suffering, but only that he
should do what benefits his patient and does no harm. Thus, the
approach that acknowledges the importance to some patients of
retaining symptoms is more in keeping with the oath than the
approach that strives to rid the patient of all symptoms.

Michael Balint summarized the doctor-patient relationship
with a nice touch:

> One of the commonest conflicts of man is caused by the discrepancy
> between his need of affection and the amount and quality of
> affection that his environment is able and willing to grant him. Some
> people fall ill to secure the attention and concern they need, and the
> illness is a claim to, a justification of, and simultaneously the
> expiation for, the extra amount of affection demanded.

Hundreds of interviews and discussions held during the preparation of this book both with hypochondriacs and physicians —specialists as well as general and family practitioners—point to the conclusion that, despite the therapeutic optimism of some writers on the subject, prognosis in the treatment of hypochondria is regarded as poor—as in Freud's time. He wrote:

> There is no doubt that there is something in these people that sets itself against their recovery, and its approach is dreaded as though it were danger. . . . The need for illness has got the upper hand in them over the desire for recovery. . . . We are dealing with what may be called a 'moral' factor, a sense of guilt, which is finding its satisfaction in the illness and refuses to give up the punishment of suffering.

In the earlier stages, these patients are usually diagnosed as suffering from anxiety neurosis or hysteria and are generally regarded as accessible to psychotherapy. Orthodox analysts believe that hypochondriacs do not form transference and treat them only if they find it possible to classify the symptoms under a more amenable syndrome. The outcome of therapy is probably in line with treatment success ratios of these conditions. Ida Macalpine and Richard Hunter—alone among psychoanalysts—believe that even the most severely affected patients can be cured or greatly helped by sympathetic and informed interviews, if attention is focused on the original body fantasies and the patient's relation to himself.

As for nonpsychiatric physicians, an informal survey conducted for the purposes of this book shows a preference for prescribing tranquilizers for hypochondriacs, followed by analgesics, and sedatives. Only two out of one hundred doctors claimed to have spent more than fifteen minutes at a time on hypochondriacs. One of these practiced in a rural area, the other was semiretired. It is clear that the economics of general practice and nonpsychiatric specialty practice do not permit the expenditure of time on counseling sessions, and that the only place a hypochondriac will be offered sufficient time, if not cure, is the

office of a psychiatrist or psychotherapist. Moreover, when
hypochondriacal patients' sensations and beliefs are misdiagnosed by a nonpsychiatric physician and treated medically and
surgically, as if they were due to physical illness, the patients will
become permanently fixed in their state by being confirmed by
medical opinion. Once this happens, psychotherapeutic approaches will become almost hopelessly difficult.

What is known about the effects, especially the effectiveness, of psychotherapy in general? Psychotherapy refers to any
treatment in which the patient or client (the designation varies
among different schools of therapy) talks to the doctor, therapist,
or counselor (again, the label varies) during a series of sessions
ranging in number from several to several hundred. In
psychotherapy, mental or emotional disturbances are treated only
through communication between patient and therapist, although
drug therapy or electric shock therapy may be administered
concurrently.

There is no conclusive evidence that psychotherapy is more
effective than general medical counseling or advice in treating
neurosis or psychosis. Strictly speaking, it cannot even be proved
that psychotherapy improves a patient's chances of recovery
beyond what they would be without any formal therapy what-
soever. Approximately two-thirds of neurotic patients will re-
cover or improve to a marked extent within about two years of
the onset of their illness, whether they are treated or not. This
figure appears to be remarkably stable from one study to another,
regardless of type of patient treated, standard of recovery
employed, or method of therapy used.

As for the psychotherapy of hypochondria, no effectiveness
studies have been performed, and informal inquiries both to
therapists and to hypochondriacs have yielded very discouraging
reports. No specific therapy has been devised for hypochondria,
and it is usually treated as anxiety neurosis. Prescriptions cover
the entire range of major and minor tranquilizers, antidepres-
sants, sedatives, and hypnotics. The interest of psychotherapists
in hypochondria is low, and their aversion to hypochondriacs

high. No other psychological disorder, with the possible exception of alcoholism, is regarded with such dim views.

(It should be noted that the drug pimozide, a tranquilizer not yet in use in the United States, has been used with success in Britain and Sweden in treating monosymptomatic [single-symptom] hypochondria. This condition is so intensely delusionary that it is often called monosymptomatic psychosis. Presenting symptoms of patients treated thus far include a complaint that an offensive bowel odor was causing social ostracism, several relating to oddness of appearance, imaginary parasitic infestation, and the case of a young man who had already had his nose fixed and then began to complain that his neck was too long. Although monosymptomatic hypochondria has been traditionally most difficult to treat, normal doses of pimozide produced rapid disappearance of the symptom in every case. Even when the delusion did not totally disappear, social adjustment improved markedly, and each patient was able to return to a much more normal life within days or weeks.)

We have concluded that the economics of nonpsychiatric practice precludes successful treatment of hypochondriacs in that setting, and we have seen that psychotherapists are either discouraged or uninterested. Still, it seems indisputable to this writer that psychotherapy can be successful if the therapist is able to lay aside personal bias and ignore the negative findings of the literature. Beginning with the premise that symptoms are always "real" to the patient, the therapist should be able to accept the hypochondriac's "unlikable" traits. True, he tends to be hypersensitive, with an underlying suspicion of others and their motivations. He is often rigid and inflexible in behavior and reacts poorly to criticism or suggestions for change. The therapist has to be able to understand that the hypochondriac feels isolated and projects onto others harmful motives and blame for his misfortune; it is his way of dealing with feelings about himself that he regards as unacceptable, demeaning, or dangerous. His behavior often causes rejection by others, which reinforces his original beliefs, but he is unable to see his own part in the cycle.

These are not pleasant traits to work with, but psychotherapists seldom complain about treating paranoid, schizophrenic, or sociopathic patients. If only they gave hypochondriacs the same patience and understanding that they give to other neurotic and psychotic patients, the outlook for successful treatment might not look so gloomy.

There are two other avenues to be explored in the treatment of hypochondria, the first of which is proper use of placebos. In general, when we think of the influence of the doctor, we usually focus on the efficacy of his therapeutic techniques. But much of the influence of the doctor on the patient is nonspecific, and results from his position of authority, suggestive powers, and influence strategies. In recent years, the study of such influences has been designated as the study of the placebo effect. The word "placebo" comes from the Latin verb, "to please," and has been defined by Arthur K. Shapiro as the "effect of any medication or procedure given with therapeutic intent, which is independent of or minimally related to the pharmacologic effect of the medication or to the specific effects of the procedure, and which operates through a psychological mechanism."

The history of medication has included such substances as dung from crocodiles, geese, and sheep; blood from bats, frogs, and turtles; oils from ants, wolves, spiders, earthworms, and the like. After reviewing the subject in detail, Shapiro concludes that ". . . we are led to the inescapable conclusion that the history of medical treatment for the most part until relatively recently is the history of the placebo effect, since almost all medications until recently were placebos."

In recent years, there has been a vast outpouring of papers documenting the significance of the placebo effect in almost every area of medical activity. One can demonstrate such effects in the treatment of almost every disease, with the exception of hypochondria, where there is a striking absence of such data. Interestingly, placebos not only lead to patient improvement, but frequently to undesirable side effects as well. Common side effects reported after the administration of placebos include drowsiness, headaches, and nervousness, and even nausea, vertigo, and gastrointestinal distress.

As to the influence of placebos, Elizabeth Beecher has collected considerable data to show that the effectiveness of a placebo is much greater when the patient is distressed than when he is not. Placebos have very little effect on relieving pain inflicted in the laboratory, but they are impressive in relieving pain after surgery, and in cases of angina, seasickness, headache, and cough. In a total of 1082 patients, Beecher found that a placebo significantly relieved pain in 35.2 percent.

Several dermatologists have reported that placebos were very effective in the treatment of the lowly wart. Of 136 cases of common wart, 44 percent were healed when painted with an inert dye, and of 43 cases of flat warts, 88 percent were cured. Since warts are a definite tissue change caused by an identifiable virus, these cures by placebo may serve as a prototype of an organic disease cured by a psychological mechanism.

Placebos have also cured more serious tissue damage than that caused by warts. Two groups of patients with bleeding peptic ulcers were compared in a municipal hospital in Budapest. The placebo group received an injection of sterile water from the doctor, who told them it was a new medicine that would produce relief. The control group received the same injection, but from nurses who told them it was an experimental medicine of undetermined effectiveness. The placebo group had excellent remissions in 70 percent of cases lasting over a period of one year, whereas the control group showed only a 25 percent rate.

It appears, in general, that placebo effects are best when those who administer inert drugs do so with authority and a confident sense of hope, and when those who receive them are emotionally aroused. The characteristics of hypochondria, together with the special qualities of the hypochondriac-doctor relationship, offer an ideal setting for a thorough study of the placebo effect in that disorder, especially in conjunction with psychotherapy.

The second avenue to be explored with at least an expectation of success is that of hypnotherapy. The suggestible hypochondriac and the authority-figure physician are a combination that offers the prospect of very fruitful experimentation, yet, to our knowledge, the technique of hypnosis has never been applied in a case of hypochondria, except when it was misdiagnosed as hysteria. Why this should be so—a question that could be used as the leitmotiv of this book—has no answer.

The suggestion that psychotherapy-*cum*-placebos and hypnotherapy may well be the most productive means of treating hypochondria is not likely to be received with jubilation by the medical community. Placebos are viewed with suspicion by most doctors, as they represent medicine's unscientific past, and are tainted with the hue of deception, however noble their purpose. As for hypnotherapy, it has always had a rocky going in the history of medicine, even though it has many well-proven medical applications. It has a certain connotation of witchcraft and magic about it, and the fact that hypnosis is now taught in a number of medical schools has not made much of an impression on the average practitioner or psychotherapist.

Meanwhile, hypochondriacs are compelled to remain in pursuit of a doctor who has an instinctive understanding of the nature of their problems and who is patient even to the point of financial sacrifice because he regards them not as crocks but as suffering human beings. There is nothing else they can do until psychotherapy abandons its present stance of negligence toward hypochondria and injects new dynamism into its approach, or until hypochondria becomes fashionable once again.

Selected Bibliography

Abadie, Jean. "L'Hypocondrie et la constitution hypocondrique." *Journal de Médecine de Bordeaux* 107 (1930): 783-91.

Adams, Robert M. *Nil: Episodes in the Literary Conquest of the Void*. New York: Oxford, 1966.

Alexander, Franz. *Psychosomatic Medicine*. New York: Norton, 1950.

Alletz, Edouard. *Maladies du siècle*. Paris: Gosselin, 1835.

Altschule, Mark David. *Roots of Modern Psychiatry*. New York: Norton, 1957.

Alvarez, Walter C. *Nervous Indigestion*. New York: Hoeber, 1931.

Anhegger, Gerda. *Der Spleen bei Charles Baudelaire*. Zurich: Fachschriften, 1937.

Areteaus: The Extant Works. Translated and edited by Francis Adams. London: Sydenham Society, 1856.

Babb, Lawrence. "The Cave of Spleen." *Review of English Studies* 12 (1939): 165-76.

————. *The Elizabethan Malady*. East Lansing: Michigan State University Press, 1951.

————. *Sanity in Bedlam*. East Lansing: Michigan State University Press, 1959.

Balint, Michael. *The Doctor, His Patient, and the Illness*. London: Pittman, 1957.

Beckett, Samuel. *The Lost Ones*. New York: Grove, 1972.

Bellak, Leopold, ed. *Psychology of Physical Illness*. New York: Grune, 1952.

Bergler, Edmund. "On the Disease-Entity Boredom (Alyosis)." *Psychiatric Quarterly* 19 (1945): 38-51.

Blackmore, Richard. *A Treatise of the Spleen and Vapours or Hypochondriacal and Hysterical Affections.* London, 1725.

Bleuler, Eugen. *Textbook of Psychiatry.* Edited by A. A. Brill. New York: Grune, 1924.

Bloomfield, Morton. *The Seven Deadly Sins: An Introduction to the History of a Religious Concept with Special Reference to Medieval English Literature.* East Lansing: Michigan State University Press, 1952.

Book, H. E. "Sexual Implications of the Nose." *Comprehensive Psychiatry* 12 (1971): 450-55.

Boswell, James. *Journals.* London, 1820.

———. *The Hypochondriack.* Edited by Margaret Bailey. Stanford: Stanford University Press, 1928.

Bouchez, Madeleine. *L'Ennui de Sénèque à Moravia.* Paris: Bordas, 1973.

Brachet, Jean-Louis. *Recherches sur l'Hystérie et l'Hypocondrie.* Paris: Gabon, 1832.

———. *Traité Complet de l'Hypocondrie.* Lyon: Savy, 1844.

Brain, Lord. "The Concept of Hysteria in the time of William Harvey." *Proceedings of the Royal Society of Medicine* 56 (1963): 317-24.

Breton, Nicholas. *Melancholike Humours with an Essay on Elizabethan Melancholy by G. B. Harrison.* London: Scholartis, 1929.

Bright, Timothy. *A Treatise of Melancholie.* London, 1586.

Briquet, Pierre. *Traité Clinique et Thérapeutique de l'Hystérie.* Paris: Ballière, 1859.

Brown, Felix. "The Bodily Complaint—a Study of Hypochondriasis." *Journal of the Mental Sciences* 82 (1936): 295-359.

Bumke, Oscar. Quoted in *Hypochondrische Syndromen,* by G. A. Ladee. Ph.D. dissertation, University of Amsterdam, 1961.

Burton, Arthur, and Adkins, Joan. "Perceived Size of Self-Image Body Parts in Schizophrenia." *Archives of General Psychiatry* 5 (1961): 131-40.

Burton, Robert. *The Anatomy of Melancholy.* New York: Tudor, 1948.

Butcher, Samuel H. *Some Aspects of the Greek Genius.* London: 1893.

Cameron, John L. *Personality Development and Psychopathology.* Boston: Houghton Mifflin, 1963.

Canter, A., et. al. "The Frequency of Physical Illness as a Function of Prior Psychological Vulnerability and Contemporary Stress." *Psychosomatic Medicine* 28 (1966): 344-50.

Cardona, Raoul. Quoted in *Hypochondrische Syndromen,* by G. A. Ladee. Ph.D. dissertation, University of Amsterdam, 1961.

Charles d'Orleans. *Poesies.* Paris: Champion, 1956.

Chastel, André. "La Melancholie de Pétrarch." *Cahiers du Sud* 38 (1953): 25-34.

Chateaubriand, François René de. *Oeuvres Romanesques.* Paris: Gallimard, 1972.

Cheyne, George. *An Essay of Health and Long Life.* London: Strahan, 1724.

————. *The English Malady.* London: Powell, 1733.

Colp, Ralph, Jr. *To Be an Invalid: The Illness of Charles Darwin.* Chicago: University of Chicago Press, 1977.

Cowden, R. C., et al. "The Use of a Physical Symptom as a Defense against Psychosis." *Journal of Abnormal and Social Psychology* 53 (1956): 133-35.

Crookshank, F. G. "Organ-Jargon." *British Journal of Medical Psychology* 10 (1930): 295-311.

Deutsch, Felix. "Psychoanalyse und Organkrankheiten." *Internazionale Zeitschrift für Psychoanalyse* 8 (1922): 290-306.

Du Laurens, André. *A Discourse of the Preservation of the Sight; of Melancholike Diseases; of Rheumes; and of Old Age.* London, 1599.

Dunbar, H. Flanders. *Emotions and Bodily Changes.* 3d ed. New York: Columbia University Press, 1946.

Engel, George L. "Studies in Ulcerative Colitis." *American Journal of Medicine* 19 (1955): 231-56.

————. "Psychogenic Pain and the Pain-Prone Patient." *American Journal of Medicine* 26 (1959): 899-918.

————. *Psychological Development in Health and Disease.* Philadelphia: Saunders, 1962.

Engel, R. L., et al. "Medical Diagnosis—Present, Past and Future." *Archives of Internal Medicine* 112 (1963): 512-19.

Esquirol, Jean-Etienne. *Des Maladies Mentales.* Paris: Ballière, 1838.

Falret, Jean-Pierre. *De l'hypocondrie et du suicide.* Paris, 1822.

Fenichel, Otto. *The Psychoanalytic Theory of Neurosis.* New York: Grune & Stratton, 1945.

Ferenczi, Sandor. "Psycho-analysis of Sexual Habits." In *Further Contributions to the Theory and Technique of Psycho-Analysis,* edited by J. Rickman. London: Gallancz, 1950.

Feuchtersleben, Ernst von. *The Principles of Medical Psychology.* Translated by H. E. Lloyd. London: Sydenham Society, 1847.

Fisher, Seymour. *Body Experience in Fantasy and Behavior.* New York: Appleton, 1970.

Flashar, Hellmut. *Melancholie und Melancholiker in den medizinischen Theorien der Antike.* Berlin: De Gruyter, 1966.

Flaubert, Gustave. *Oeuvres.* Lausanne: Editions Rencontre, 1965.

Freud, Sigmund. "On the Grounds for Detaching a Particular Syndrome from Neurasthenia under the Description 'Anxiety Neurosis.' " *The Complete Psychological Works of Sigmund Freud,* 24 vols., edited and translated by James Strachey. Standard edition, Vol. 3. New York: Norton, 1976.

————. "Contributions to a Discussion on Masturbation." Standard edition, Vol. 12. New York: Norton, 1976

————. "On Narcissism: an Introduction." Standard edition, Vol. 14. New York: Norton, 1976.

Gellert Lyons, Bridget. *Voices of Melancholy: Studies in Literary Treatments of Melancholy in Renaissance England.* London: Routledge, 1971.

Gide, André. *Romans.* Paris: Gallimard, 1958.

Gillespie, R. D. "Hypochondria." *Guy's Hospital Reports* 78 (1928): 408-60.

Grace, William J., et al. *The Human Colon.* New York: Harper's, 1951.

Greenberg, H. Phillip. "Hypochondriasis." *Medical Journal of Australia* 47 (1960): 763-67.

Greenfield, N. S., et al. "Hypochondriasis." *Journal of Nervous and Mental Diseases* 126 (1958): 482-84.

Griesinger, Wilhelm. *Die Pathologie und Therapie der psychischen Krankheiten.* Stuttgart: Krabbe, 1845.

Grinker, Roy R. *Psychosomatic Research.* New York: Norton, 1953.

―――. *Psychosomatic Casebook.* Philadelphia: Blakiston, 1954.

Gull, Sir William. *A Collection of the Public Writings of Sir William Gull.* London, 1894.

Hackett, Thomas, et al. "Psychiatric Management of Operative Syndromes." *Psychosomatic Medicine* 22 (1960): 267, 356.

Henne, Michel. "L'hypocondrie a travers d'ages." *Histoire de la Médecine* 5 (1955): 5-27.

Hes, J. "Hypochondriasis in Oriental Jewish Immigrants." *Journal of Social Psychiatry* 4 (1958): 18-23

Higier, H. "Hypochondria iatrogenetica." *Zentralblatt für Neurologie und Psychiatrie* 51 (1929): 690-94.

Hinkle, L. E., et al. "An Investigation of the Relation Between Life Experience, Personality Characteristics, and General Susceptibility to Illness." *Psychosomatic Medicine* 20 (1958): 278-94.

Hippocrates. *The Genuine Works of Hippocrates.* Translated by Francis Adams. New York: Wood, 1886.

Hubble, Donald. "The Life of the Shawl." *Lancet* 2 (1953): 1351-54.

Hunt, Robert C. "The Psyche as an Object of Hypochondriacal Preoccupation." *Psychiatric Quarterly* 14 (1940): 490-95.

Hutchison, Richard. "Hypochondriasis." *British Medical Journal* 1 (1934): 365-67.

Jahrreiss, Wilhelm. "Das hypochondrische Denken." *Archives der Psychiatrie und Nervenkrankheiten* 92 (1930): 686-861.

James, Irving P. "On Hypochondriasis." *Medical Journal of Australia* 47 (1960): 521-25.

Janet, Pierre. *Ètat Mental des Histériques*. Paris: Rueff, 1892.

Jankélévitch, Vladimir. *L'Aventure, l'Ennui et le Sérieux*. Paris: Aubier, 1963.

Jolly, Hans, and Hitzig, Paul. Quoted in *Hypochondrische Syndromen*. Ph.D. dissertation, University of Amsterdam, 1961.

Kahana, Robert J. "Studies in Medical Psychology." *Psychiatry and Medicine* 3 (1972): 1-22.

Kasl, S. V., et al. "Health Behavior, Illness Behavior, and Sick-Role Behavior." *Archives of Environmental Health* 12 (1966): 246-66, 531-41.

Katzenellenbogen, Solomon. "Hypochondriacal Complaints." *American Journal of Psychiatry* 98 (1942): 815-22.

Kenyon, F. E. "Hypochondriasis: A Clinical Study." *British Journal of Psychiatry* 110 (1964): 478-88.

————. "Hypochondriasis: A Survey of Some Historical, Clinical and Social Aspects." *British Journal of Medical Psychology* 38 (1965): 117-33.

Kierkegaard, Søren. *Fear and Trembling*. Princeton, N. J.: Princeton University Press, 1941.

Kraepelin, Emil. *Psychiatrie*. Leipzig: Barth, 1915.

Kuhn, Reinhard. "Ennui in der französischen Literatur." *Die Neueren Sprachen* 1 (1967): 17-30.

————. *The Demon of Noontide*. Princeton, N. J.: Princeton University Press, 1976.

Lachman, Sheldon J. "A Behavioristic Rationale for the Development of Psychosomatic Phenomena." *Journal of Psychology* 56 (1963): 230-48.

Ladee, G. A. *Hypochondrische Syndromen.* Ph.D. dissertation, University of Amsterdam, 1961.

LeGall, Béatrice. *L'Imaginaire chez Senancour.* Paris: Corti, 1966.

Leonhard, Karl. "On the Treatment of Ideo-hypochondriasis." *International Journal of Social Psychiatry* 7 (1961): 123-33.

Levy, David M. "Body Interest in Children and Hypochondria." *American Journal of Psychiatry* 89 (1932): 295-315.

Lipowski, Zbigniew J., ed. *Psychosomatic Aspects of Physical Illness.* Advances in Psychosomatic Medicine, vol. 8. Basel: Karger, 1972.

————. "Psychosomatic Medicine in a Changing Society." *Comprehensive Psychiatry* 14 (1973): 203-15.

Lipsitt, Don R. "Medical and Psychological Characteristics of Crocks." *Psychiatry and Medicine* 1 (1970): 15-25.

Ludwig, E. G., et al. Self-perception of Sickness and the Seeking of Medical Care." *Journal of Health and Social Behavior* 10 (1969): 125-33.

Mabry, J. H. "Lay Concepts of Etiology." *Journal of Chronic Diseases* 17 (1964): 371-86.

Macalpine, Ida, and Hunter, Richard A. *Schizophrenia.* London: Routledge, 1956.

MacBryde, Cyril M., and Blacklow, Robert S., eds. *Signs and Symptoms.* 5th ed. Philadelphia: Lippincott, 1970.

McCranie, E. James. "The Hypochondriacal Patient." *Female Patient* 1 (1978): 108-11.

McKinley, John C., et al. "A Multiphasic Personality Schedule. II. A Differential Study of Hypochondriasis." *Journal of Psychology* 10 (1940): 255-68.

Mandeville, Bernard de. *A Treatise of the Hypochondriack and Hysterick Passions.* London: Towson, 1730.

Marks, Geoffrey, and Beatty, William. *Epidemics.* New York: Scribner, 1976.

Mechanic, David. "The Concept of Illness Behavior." *Journal of Chronic Diseases* 15 (1962): 189-94.
———. *Medical Sociology*. New York: Free Press, 1968.
Miles, H. W., et al. *Case Histories in Psychosomatic Medicine*. New York: Norton, 1952.
Montégut, Emile. "Les confidences d'un hypocondriaque." In his *Types litteraires*. Paris, 1882.

Painter, George D. *Marcel Proust, A Biography*. 2 vols. New York: Vintage, 1978.
Paul, Leonard. "Psychosomatic Aspects of Low Back Pain: A Review." *Psychosomatic Medicine* 12 (1950): 116-24.
Paulus Aegineta. *The Seven Books of Paulus Aegineta*. Translated by Francis Adams. London: Sydenham Society, 1844.
Pilowsky, I. "Primary and Secondary Hypochondriasis." *Acta Psychiatrica Scandinavica* 46 (1970): 273-85.
Pinel, Philippe. *A Treatise on Insanity*. Translated by D. D. Davis. London: Cadell, 1806.
Preston, Mary I. "Physical Complaints Without Organic Basis." *Journal of Pediatrics* 17 (1940): 279-304.

Richards, Esther Loring. "The Significance and Management of Hypochondriacal Trends in Children." *New York State Journal of Mental Hygiene* 7 (1923): 43-69.
———. "Following the Hypochondriacal Child for a Decade." *Journal of Pediatrics* 18 (1941): 528-37.
Rickels, K., et al. "Personality Differences Between Somatically and Psychologically Oriented Neurotic Patients." *Journal of Nervous and Mental Diseases* 142 (1966): 10-18.
Robinson, Nicholas. *A New System of the Spleen, Vapours, and Hypochondriack Melancholy* . . . London: Bettersworth, 1739.
Romains, Jules. *Knock, ou le Triomphe de la Médecine*. Paris: Editions de la Nouvelle Révue Francaise, 1924.
Rosen, George. "People, Disease and Emotion." *Bulletin of the History of Medicine* 41 (1967): 9-20.

Rosenfeld, Harold. "Some Observations on the Psychopathology of Hypochondriacal States." *International Journal of Psychoanalysis* 39 (1958): 121-24.

Ross, T. A. "Discussion on Hypochondria." *Proceedings of the Royal Society of Medicine* 22 (1928): 176-82.

Sartre, Jean-Paul. *L'Idiot de la Famille: Gustave Flaubert de 1821 à 1857.* Paris: Gallimard, 1972.

Schilder, Paul. *The Image and Appearance of the Human Body.* New York: International Universities Press, 1950.

Schlaegel, Thomas F. *Psychosomatic Ophthalmology.* Baltimore: Williams & Wilkins, 1957.

Selye, Hans. "The General Adaptation Syndrome and the Diseases of Adaptation." *Clinical Endocrinology* 6 (1946): 117-28.

Sena, J. F. *A Bibliography of Melancholy, 1660-1800.* London: Nether, 1970.

Sénancour, Etienne de. *Obermann.* Paris: Arthaud, 1947.

Shapiro, Arthur K. "A Contribution to the History of the Placebo Effect." *Behavioral Sciences,* May 1960, 109-35.

Shontz, Frank C. *Perceptual and Cognitive Aspects of Body Experience.* New York: Academic Press. 1969.

Silverman, Samuel. *Psychological Aspects of Physical Symptoms.* New York: Appleton, 1968.

Sperling, Michael. "Transference Neurosis in Patients with Psychosomatic Disorders." *Psychoanalytic Quarterly* 36 (1967): 342-55.

Stoeckle, John D., et al. "On Going to See the Doctor—the Contributions of the Patient to the Decision to Seek Medical Aid." *Journal of Chronic Diseases* 16 (1963): 975-89.

Sulzberger, Morton B. and Wolf, J. "The Treatment of Warts by Suggestion." *Medical Record* 140 (1934): 552-56.

Sweetland, Allan. "Hypnotic Neuroses: Hypochondria and Depression." *Journal of General Psychology* 39 (1948): 91-105.

Sydenham, Thomas. *The Works of Thomas Sydenham, M.D.* London: Sydenham Society, 1848.

Tuke, Daniel Hack. *A Dictionary of Psychological Medicine.* Philadelphia: Blakiston, 1892.

Veith, Ilza. "On Hysterical and Hypochondriacal Afflictions." *Bulletin of the History of Medicine* 30 (1956): 233-40.

Wahl, Charles W. "Unconscious Factors in the Psychodynamics of the Hypochondriacal Patient." *Psychosomatics* 4 (1963) 9-14.

Walton, Izaak. *Lives.* Edited by George Saintsbury. Oxford, 1927.

Wenzel, Siegfried. "Petrarch's Accidia." *Studies in the Renaissance* 7 (1961): 36-48.

Whytt, Robert. *Observations on Nervous, Hypochondriack and Hysterick Disorders.* Edinburgh: Becket, 1764.

Willis, Thomas. *The London Practice of Physick, or the Whole Practical Part of Physick Contained in the Works of Dr. Willis.* London: Basset, 1685.

Wolff, Harold G. "A Concept of Disease in Man." *Psychosomatic Medicine* 24 (1962): 25-30.

―――. *Stress and Disease.* Edited by S. Wolf and H. Goodell. Springfield, Ill.: Thomas, 1967.

Wolf, Stewart, and Wolff, Harold G. *Human Gastric Function.* New York: Oxford, 1947.

Wolf, Stewart, et al. *Life Stress and Essential Hypertension.* Baltimore: Williams & Wilkins, 1955.

Zabarenko, Richard N., et al. "The Psychodynamics of Physicianhood." *Psychiatry* 33 (1970): 102-18.

Zaidens, Samuel H. "Dermatologic Hypochondriasis." *Psychosomatic Medicine* 12 (1950): 250-53.

Zola, Irving K. "Culture and Symptoms: an Analysis of Patients' Presenting Problems." *American Sociology Review* 31 (1966): 615-30.

INDEX

Abadie, Jean, 50
acedia (accidie), 73-4
adaptation
  biological, 11-12
  and illness, 10-11
Addison, Joseph, 80
aging, 61-2
Alexander, Franz, 17-19, 36
American Journal of Psychotherapy,
  30
Anatomie of the Minde (Rogers), 86
Anatomy of Melancholy, The (Burton),
  33, 68
anorexia nervosa, 158
anxiety, 14, 45
  and hypochondria, 97-8
Aretaeus, 32, 97
Aristotle, 69, 70
arthritis, rheumatoid, 17
As You Like It (Shakespeare), 77-8
Asher, Richard, 157-9
asthma, bronchial, 17, 18-19
Avicenna, 99
Aymara Indians, 11

Babb, Lawrence, 76, 96
Balint, Michael, 174
Baudelaire, Charles, 69, 74
Beckett, Samuel, 75, 106
Beecher, Elizabeth, 179
Being and Nothingness (Sartre), 69
Bernard, Claude, 10-11
bile, black
  as melancholy, 69-70, 88
bile, yellow (choler), 69
Birth of Tragedy, The (Nietzsche), 73
Blackmore, Richard, 32
Bleuler, Eugen, 34
body
  communication function of, 42-3
  delusions of, 14, 37-8
  and emotional arousal, 14, 25-6
  fluids of, 69
  perceptions of, 44-6
  preoccupation with, 14, 33, 37, 56, 59

  see also body image; mind-body
    dichotomy body image
  disturbances of, 14-15, 41-6
Boswell, James, 29, 71-2
Breuer, Josef, 41
Bright, Timothy, 67, 92
Briquet, Pierre, 100
British Medical Dictionary
  definition of illness of, 9-10
Brown, Sir Walter Langdon, 109
Bumke, Oscar, 55, 63-4
Burns, Robert, 67
Burton, Robert, 33, 38, 68, 84, 87, 88,
  89, 91, 95, 99, 156
Butcher, Samuel H., 72

Cameron, John L., 36-7
Cardona, Raoul, 57-8
Cellars of the Vatican, The (Gide), 105
Charcot, Jean-Martin, 32, 100
Chekhov, Anton, 16
Cheyne, George, 68, 80, 96, 97, 98
Chicago Institute of Psychoanalysis, 17
choler; *see* bile, yellow
Cicero, Marcus Tullius, 72
closet hypochondria, 30-1, 62-3, 148-54
colitis, ulcerative, 17, 18
complexion
  Elizabethan classification of, 83-4
Concerning the Tranquility of the Soul
  (Seneca), 70-2
conversion, 14, 42
Culpepper, Samuel, 31
cultural beliefs
  and health and illness, 12-13

dancing mania, 21-2
Darwin, Charles, 19-21
De l'hypocondrie et du suicide (Falret),
  33
De Vita (Ficino), 87
definitions
  of health and illness, 9-10
  of hypochondria, 54-66
Delmas, P., 50